The Practitioner's Raindrop Resource Guide

Confidently Tailor Raindrop To Serve A Wider Variety Of Clients And Excel In This Technique!

Christina G. Hagan M.Ed, LCCI, LMBT

Adapting Raindrop

Do you have a goal to grow your Raindrop practice?

The best way to do that is to help your Raindrop Receivers to see the value of their sessions with you.

Join me in a free video program where I'll share with you how to involve your Receivers in their Raindrop so they want to come back for more!

I know you'll be thrilled to see how the tailoring information discussed in Part One will help you to grow your Raindrop Practice.

**View the videos here:
https//:AdaptingRaindrop.com/Value/**

The Practitioner's Raindrop Resource Guide©
Copyright 2023
Christina G. Hagan

All rights reserved. No part of this publication may be reproduced, distributed or transmitted in any form or by any means, including photocopying, recording, or other electronic or mechanical methods, without the prior written permission of the publisher, except in the case of brief quotations embodied in critical reviews and certain other noncommercial uses permitted by copyright law.

Although the author and publisher have made every effort to ensure that the information in this book was correct at press time, the author and publisher do not assume and hereby disclaim any liability to any party for any loss, damage, or disruption caused by errors or omissions, whether such errors or omissions result from negligence, accident, or any other cause.

Adherence to all applicable laws and regulations, including international, federal, state and local governing professional licensing, business practices, advertising, and all other aspects of doing business in the US, Canada or any other jurisdiction is the sole responsibility of the reader and consumer.

Neither the author nor the publisher assumes any responsibility or liability whatsoever on behalf of the consumer or reader of this material. Any perceived slight of any individual or organization is purely unintentional.

The resources in this book are provided for informational purposes only and should not be used to replace the specialized training and professional judgment of a health care or mental health care professional.

Neither the author nor the publisher can be held responsible for the use of the information provided within this book. Please always consult a trained professional before making any decision regarding treatment of yourself or others.

ISBN (ebook): 979-8-88759-609-9

ISBN (paperback): 979-8-88759-608-2

Dedication

This book is dedicated to all those Raindrop Professionals who decided to follow their heart and take the road less traveled.

You fell in love with this technique and chose to create a wellness practice using a tool that many are unfamiliar with. Those who, like you, see the numerous benefits of Raindrop are also in a learning phase.

There is still so much to learn about all the ways the essential oils and this technique may support us.

That is exciting and frustrating at the same time as no one has all the answers.

Congratulations to you Raindropper, because you are part of the few who are becoming the leaders in the new wellness frontier!

Table of Contents

Introduction 9

Part One The Basic Recipe **17**

Chapter 1:   How Raindrop Supports Us 19

Chapter 2:   The Basic Recipe. 25

Chapter 3:   Adding Other Oils 45

Chapter 4:   Replacing an Oil 49

Chapter 5:   An Emotional Release Raindrop 57

Chapter 6:   Adding More Massage to Your Raindrop. 61

Chapter 7:   All About the Base 63

Chapter 8:   Some more about detoxing. 65

Part Two Receiver Comfort **69**

Chapter 9:   A Sitting Raindrop. 71

Chapter 10: Giving Raindrop Side-Lying 81

Chapter 11: Spinal VitaFlex on the Feet when Sitting. 87

Chapter 12: Stuffy Sinuses 91

Chapter 13: Muscle Cramps - What to Do and How to Avoid Them. 97

Chapter 14: Prone to Sitting 105

Part Three Special Considerations **107**

Amputation. 110

Autism. 110

Babies and Toddlers. 111

Brain 114

Cancer. 114

Children 120

Cortisone Injections for Pain. 120

Edema vs Lymphedema 121

Emotional Release and Trauma Response. 122

Multiple Sclerosis (MS) and Other Conditions Affecting the Myelin Sheath 125

Neuropathy 126

Nursing 126

Obesity 128

Pregnancy 128

Scoliosis. 131

Chapter 15: A Growing Resource 133

Acknowledgments. 135

References 137

Author Bio 137

Introduction

Why I Wrote this Book

A long, long time ago when I graduated as a teacher for the Blind and Visually Impaired and as an Orientation and Mobility Instructor, I knew that I would be the BEST teacher for the blind (besides Mary Ingels from *The Little House on the Prairie* book series). As I packed my bags for my first job, I couldn't wait to help my students gain functional independence skills.

When I started my first teaching job I had the realization that my goal may have some challenges. I wanted to be this amazing teacher, yet I was finding myself alone, with very few people to ask for guidance.

You see, I was an itinerant teacher, which meant that I traveled from school to school to see my students. Since visual impairment is a low incidence disability, there was often only one student who was visually impaired in the whole school I was visiting.

Not only did I put a crazy amount of mileage on my car, but I quickly learned that I was often the only teacher in the school that had any training or background working with a student with a visual impairment. That meant that everyone who worked with that student looked to me for answers when it came to teaching this student.

At some of the larger districts where I worked, there were other Teachers of the Visually Impaired, and I was super excited to mentor with them. I thought I would finally get the chance to talk with another teacher who knew about Visual Impairment too, someone who was familiar with the terminology, the technology, the common challenges, and maybe the solutions! Disappointed again, I found that since we were all on the road working with students, our time together to talk, compare notes, and ask for advice was severely limited.

Being that I wanted to do the best that I could for my students, I put all my energies into finding solutions on my own. My students and I did a lot of trouble shooting together until we found a solution to a problem or a method that worked for them.

As things in my life changed, I ended up working at The Rehab Center for the Blind as an Orientation and Mobility Instructor. There I met Patty, another Mobility Instructor. She took me under her wing and shared with me her years of experience, which helped me to start my job without reinventing the teaching wheel. She showed me the best intersections to practice street crossings, the friendliest bus routes, and the companies with the best low-vision aids. She was happy to give me advice about teaching techniques whenever I asked.

This support helped me to be a better teacher right away because I didn't have to do the hunting and searching, and thus I could focus more on my students. Her assistance allowed me to succeed and thrive.

I share this story with you because I have a feeling this is how you may feel about the Raindrop Technique with your Raindrop Receivers.

When you came out of your Raindrop training, I bet you were excited and your heart was full. You knew that you would be doing Raindrop sessions for your current and future clients, offering them peace, relaxation, and solutions to physical and/or emotional concerns.

You jumped into your training with the intention of helping and healing many people, and then when the training was completed and you had your certification or license, you looked around and realized…you were the only one in your town that offered this amazing essential oil technique. You didn't have anyone to ask for advice. You couldn't have coffee with a peer to find out how they chose to work with Receivers with a certain wellness concern. Who could you turn to for advice? Where could you go to learn more?

You might have felt alone, but because you are passionate about helping people, you kept on going, doing Raindrops and trouble shooting on your own.

My experience as a new Vision Teacher helped me to understand the need for continued guidance, support, and community for my Raindrop students. Moreover, my relationship with Patty showed me how drastically mentorship reduces the learning curve, which helps someone excel in their field.

I want to be your Patty and share with you what I've learned these past ten plus years to help reduce your learning curve so that you can shine in this field. That is why I started Adapting Raindrop, which offers online education, coaching, educational memberships, and books, like this one!

Who is this book for?

Originally, when this book was just an idea in my head, I was going to write two books, one for Massage Therapists and one for Spiritual/Emotional Healers. This distinction was based on the fact that both professions focus on different facets of the body: physical versus emotional and spiritual.

Talking to both groups in one book seemed challenging at first, but then I realized that whether you are a Spiritual Healer, Massage Therapist, Chiropractor, Nurse, or Energy Worker, we all have the same issues to consider when seeking to help our clients. These include detoxing, choosing different oils for tailored support, keeping clients comfortable, and adhering to special considerations. All of those issues will be covered in this book. Most of these concerns will be universal, and all wellness practitioners who offer Raindrop as part of their wellness services will benefit from learning these concepts, as will their Raindrop Receivers.

Physical or Emotional?

When I think of essential oil use or Raindrop, I always see two parts of the practice: the support they give us emotionally and spiritually, and the benefits they offer us physically. Deciding on which part you are going to focus on depends on what your goals are. Your goals, in turn, are determined by who is giving the Raindrop (you and your business) and who is receiving the Raindrop.

One evening as I was cooking dinner and looking at a pile of potatoes on the kitchen counter, I had a light bulb moment about Raindrop and the difference in physical or emotional support it offers. My family loves potatoes. We eat them a lot, so I prepare them for us in many different ways. As I prepared them that evening, I realized that the potatoes are like the Raindrop Technique and the knife is equivalent to you and your practice. You can use the knife to slice the potatoes into wedges, toss them with oil and spices, and put them in the air fryer for crispy potato wedges to eat with dinner. Or you can chop the potatoes into tiny pieces and fry them up with butter in a pan to make hash browns to eat with eggs for breakfast. The potato is the same, it is the intention of the chef using the tool that changes the outcome.

The same is true for Raindrop. The outcome of the Raindrop session will be determined by who is giving the Raindrop and what they are trying to achieve based on the desired goals of the Receiver.

A Massage Therapist like me focuses on the physical aspects of our clients, like relieving tight muscles, providing relaxation, or supporting detoxing goals. This means that our Raindrop Receivers are going to look for the physical support that their Raindrop session offers them.

A Spiritual Healer is focused on emotions, energy, spirituality, forgiveness, and God. A Raindrop from a Spiritual Healer will be a totally different experience than a Raindrop from a Massage Therapist as they will have a different focus and approach to health and wellness, and therefore, their Raindrop Sessions.

This Resource Guide will help you to refine your Receivers' goals so you can develop a unique, tailored Raindrop experience specific to their current needs. You will learn concepts that will help you to be more intentional with your tool (Raindrop). You will also learn how to keep all of your Receivers as comfortable as possible as you give them their Raindrop, even those who are unable to lie on a massage table.

Two Halves of the Same Coin

You and I both know that many physical and emotional aspects of wellness blend together. You can't be a Raindropper and totally ignore the other half of healing. It just doesn't work that way. A Massage Therapist offering Raindrop to their clients should discuss the possibility of emotional release, even though their focus may be physical. If, as a Massage Therapist, you become interested in working with clients in the emotional/spiritual realm, then fabulous! Let's first make sure you have the support of additional education in that area and the licensing, too.

The same goes for a Spiritual/Emotional Healer. As a Spiritual Healer is applying oils with the intention of emotional support, you also know that these oils are great for supporting the muscular system, too. As you give the Raindrop you may notice that your Receiver has some majorly tight muscles. If the session with you does not alleviate the tightness, you should refer this client to a Massage Therapist. If you, as a Spiritual Healer, find that you really enjoy working on the body and want to add massage to your practice, then wonderful! It is time to then gain the support of additional education and licensing to do so confidently and legally.

In time, I foresee healers like us (Massage Therapists and Spiritual Healers) to be practicing in both realms. I feel that eventually the idea of emotions affecting our physical health will not be such a new and "far-fetched" idea, and the roles of Massage Therapists and Spiritual Healers will be blended into one. Therapists may gravitate towards one side, emotional or physical, but the concepts and ideas will be used in tandem. The transition between physical and emotional support during a session will blend uniquely based on that client's needs and the therapist's skills.

I love and appreciate both sides of this wellness coin. During my sixteen years of bodywork and Raindrop, my view and practice have changed from being purely physical to a blended approach, and many of my clients have been very open to this combination.

I hope this book supports all my fellow professionals offering Raindrop in their wellness practice, no matter where their focus lies on the physical or emotional wellness line.

I wish I could ask Gary Young His Thoughts

Some people I know feel that the Raindrop Technique, as designed by Gary Young, is a complete modality and does not need any adapting or changing in any way. From what I understand, as Gary was demonstrating the technique to others at meetings, trainings, and conventions, he changed the Raindrop to fit the person on whom he was demonstrating. He often forgot that he was supposed to be in "teacher mode" during these demonstrations and went into "healer mode."

This is why Gary would do one set of oils or different techniques each time he demonstrated Raindrops.

This inconsistency led to some confusion and discord when people debated the best way to do Raindrop, arguing that *"this* is the way Gary taught it."

In his book *Essential Oils Integrative Medical Guide*, there is a chapter about Raindrop with pictures and directions (*Essential Oils Integrative Medical Guide, pp. 228*). It is often overlooked, but it gives us insight into one of the ways Gary Young was showing how Raindrop can be adapted.

We'll discuss all the ways one can add to or change up the oils used in Raindrop in Chapters Three and Four.

A Brief Overview

This resource guide is divided up into three parts. In Part One we will cover what I call The Basic Recipe for Raindrop and how that recipe can be adapted to fit your Receivers' current needs.

We will also discuss detoxing. One of the beauties of Raindrop is its cleansing and detoxing capabilities, but that can be its downfall, too. We will go over how to detox gently, with grace, instead of unintentionally and unexpectedly having too strong of a detox.

We will walk through how to add other essential oils to Raindrop to support the receiver either physically or emotionally. In this section, you will also learn how to find a substitute oil if you don't have that oil on hand or if someone is allergic to an oil.

As you get more comfortable with the idea of modifying Raindrop, we will look at how to replace some of the essential oils used in The Basic Recipe of Raindrop. I'll show you my "System Supporting Raindrop" chart, which will guide you in creating a Raindrop designed to support a specific system. I'll also share my "Emotional Release Raindrop" protocol.

In Part Two we will focus on how to keep your Receiver comfortable. You'll learn about different options for giving a Raindrop if your Receiver can't lie on a massage table prone (face down) or supine (face up). This section will also show you what to do if your Receiver is super stuffy from lying face down for so long, has leg cramps, or if their back starts hurting while they are on your massage table.

I've added many pictures in Part Two and I do my best to explain and describe how to make these adaptations. If pictures are really "worth a thousand words," then videos must be worth at least a million! I have given you the option of requesting access to videos that demonstrate each adaptation which may be helpful in understanding the finer points and details.

Part Three is all about special considerations of your Receivers. As a practitioner, I want this book to be a tool that you can reach for whenever you need it. You'll find all the Special Considerations in alphabetical order for easy reference.

This segment is where I expect this resource guide will grow and develop as more people share with me what they have done that has been helpful for their Receivers. I get so excited at the idea that this will be an evolving resource guide for you and me. If you have found a tip or method that works great with a specific type of client, please contact me at AdaptingRaindrop.com to share your insight. I'd love to add your nugget of wisdom in the *Raindrop Resource Guide* or *All Things Raindrop* to support others practicing Raindrop, along with giving you credit.

PART ONE
The Basic Recipe

How Raindrop Supports Us 19

The Basic Recipe 23

Adding Other Oils 43

Replacing an Oil 47

An Emotional Release Raindrop 55

Adding More Massage to Your Raindrop 59

All About the Base 61

Some more about detoxing 63

CHAPTER ONE
How Raindrop Supports Us

Raindrop supports us in so many ways! Sometimes it can be overwhelming to keep track of the number of ways we can receive support from the oils.

The Nerve Subway

You know we can use essential oils by inhaling them, rubbing them on our skin, and taking them by mouth to help us internally. I feel Raindrop is another type of application method entirely. Why do you think we drop oils on the spine and then spend all that time feathering? It is not just because it spreads the oils and helps with relaxation.

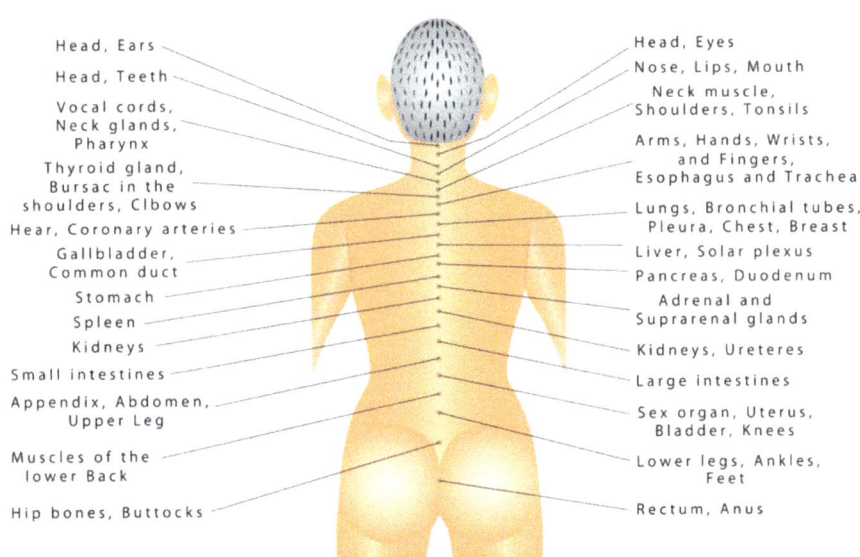

Look at the spine, and notice how the nerves exit the spine and travel through the body to innervate or support various organs, systems, or muscle groups in your body.

The molecules of essential oils are tiny, electrically charged molecules that are transdermal. This means that these molecules are absorbed into your body very quickly. Once these oil molecules are absorbed, they enter your blood, lymph, cells, and nerves.

In Raindrop, the essential oils are applied or dropped onto the spine, and then "feathered" in. The feathering stimulates all the nerves exiting the spine.

Being that essential oil molecules are electrical in nature, the theory is that they can travel along the nerves and are "delivered" to the organs, systems, and muscles that the nerves innervate, which is why we stimulate them with the feathering technique.

Very similar to a subway, the nerve carries the essential oil molecule right to the system or organ that the nerve supports. When we apply oils on the spine, as in Raindrop, we are using this quick and efficient delivery system.

How cool is it that each oil used in The Basic Recipe supports a different system of the body? By following The Basic Recipe, you are giving your Receiver full-body support.

Oil	Supports
Valor	Balance Energies
Oregano	Immune System
Thyme	Immune System
Basil	Muscular System
Wintergreen	Skeletal System
Marjoram	Involuntary and Voluntary Muscles
Cypress	Circulatory and Lymph Systems
Peppermint	Digestive, Respiratory, Nervous Systems

We also have the option of choosing which system we would like to support. I'll go into more details on that in Chapter Four.

But Wait… There's More!

As if giving the body full support through Raindrop isn't enough, there are quite a few other ways that Raindrop physically supports our Receivers. Included below are a few additional ways essential oils may offer our bodies opportunities to heal.

Essential oils have a positive affect on our general health by changing our pH levels. In Dr. Stewart's book *The Chemistry of Essential Oils Made Simple*, he explains that "…even though essential oils are neither alkaline or acid in and of themselves, their effect upon a person is to alkalize their bodies and move them toward a higher state of health and wellness" (page 350).

Essential oils are also great at making our bodies an unfriendly environment to microbes, acting as a great immune booster.

The phenols are ninja masters at cleansing receptor sites on our cells, which can be considered part of a detox. When those receptor sites are clean, the cells in the body will have better communication with each other, which translates to better health.

Phenol molecules don't stop at clearing our receptor sites; they are also skilled at breaking down toxic loads in all the places that the body stores it.

It is not just the phenols that have a positive effect on our receptor sites, but "…terpenes are able to change the expression of receptors, meaning that they are able to alter the amount of receptors present on the cell surface, either increasing or decreasing them" (*Medical Aromatherapy, Healing with Essential Oils* by Kurt Schnaubelt, page 98).

Essential oil molecules can be antispasmodic and reduce inflammation, which can help reduce pain in voluntary muscles and support correct function of involuntary muscles.

One of the reasons Raindrop and essential oils can be so relaxing is that some of the molecules can bring balance to the autonomic nervous system, supporting relaxation.

Each essential oil has a unique frequency, as does each organ in your body. The interaction of frequencies between oils and cells offers us additional physical and spiritual wellness support.

The Emotional and Spiritual Aspects of Raindrop

A Raindrop Practitioner or Licensed Spiritual Healer knows that each essential oil not only supports the body physically, but also emotionally or spiritually. Each time we drop an oil we need to remember that the support that is being offered covers all of these different aspects of our Receivers. When you are reaching for your oils, you may have a different intent in mind depending on the needs of your Receiver.

The beauty of these essential oils lies in the fact that each oil and blend has a unique frequency. Emotions have unique frequencies, too. It is the vibrational concert between the emotions that our physical and energetic body are holding on to and the frequency of the essential oils that creates or causes emotional release.

In my head, I see a scene of vibrating essential oil molecules dancing and singing to our DNA, receptor sites, cells, and chakras. Our body responds to vibrations and so do the trapped emotions or energy. The melody that the essential oil molecules and emotional energy bundles are singing to each other will change depending on what the body decides it needs at the time. Sometimes the song can be gentle and soothing, other times aggressive and heated.

If you are observant, you can see and sense this vibrational concert being played out both in and on your Receiver's body. The Receiver's skin, breathing, posture, and verbal feedback will give you information on what part of the vibrational song is being sung. Likewise, you may receive suggestions from the Holy Spirit, intuition, books, spirit guides, or other forms of guidance. Based on this information, you may decide to add other oils, pray, state affirmations, or add other modalities.

Things to Keep in Mind

Whether you and your Receiver are focused on the physical aspects of Raindrop or the emotional healing one may receive, it is important to keep in mind that the oils are always working on a "cleansing" level. They do an amazing job at detoxing the body. But is having a big detox the number one goal for your Receiver during a session? It may not be! Therefore, it is important for you to be familiar with each oil and its supportive qualities, which we will discuss in the following chapter.

CHAPTER TWO
The Basic Recipe

When talking about Raindrop, there is a basic set of oils used, which I call The Basic Recipe. They address all the systems of the body and offer a beautiful combination of phenols, monoterpenes, and sesquiterpenes. These are three main molecules found in essential oils that help us receive the physical support and healing that Raindrop offers.

Here's a quick break down of the general quality of these molecules:

Phenols

- Clean off the receptor sites in our cells, dislodging toxins, sugar, and the "yuck" we are exposed to in our modern world
- Fight invaders (viruses, bacteria, yeast)
- Support our immune system

Monoterpenes

- Gently cleanse
- Support healing
- Balance
- Relieves pain

Sesquiterpenes

- Oxygenate
- Elevate moods
- Have calming capabilities

If you look at the oils that are used in The Basic Recipe, you'll see there are a lot of cleansers used.

Oil	P, M or S
Valor	Monoterpenes & Sesquiterpenes
Oregano	Phenols
Thyme	Phenols
Basil	Phenols
Wintergreen	Phenols
Marjoram	Monoterpenes
Cypress	Monoterpenes & Sesquiterpenes
Peppermint	Phenols

Cleaning is a good thing. We want to cleanse and detox our bodies. The cleansing of our receptor sites on our cells allows our cells to receive information from messenger-carrying molecules floating around our bodies. When we have good communication between the organs and cells of our bodies, we have health, and that is our goal, right? Physical toxins may not be the only thing "clogging" those receptor sites. There may be emotional toxins too, which are released by a phenolic molecule.

A common mistake I see when people use The Basic Recipe (even with the greatest of intentions) is they unknowingly detox their Receiver too much, too fast which can lead to an uncomfortable and unpleasant experience.

Is Our Receiver Ready for a Detox?

When people are detoxing, they can often experience a headache, skin rash, upset stomach, or diarrhea. These are known as Herxheimer reactions, or a healing crisis.

While I personally consider detoxing to be a good thing, it is important to ask if the Receiver is expecting a detox. Did they come to see you for a detox or just to relax? You need to know what their goals are and if they are prepared for the possibility of a detox.

As someone who offers Raindrop, I feel it is of utmost importance that we respect the goals and intention of our Receiver. I also feel that we need to take into consideration that many people are toxic and don't know it. Just asking someone, "Are you carrying a toxic load?" most likely will not give you the information that you are looking for. You need to ask questions with intention behind them.

As essential oils are becoming more popular and widely used, so is Raindrop. That means we need to gain information from the Receiver so we have a greater chance of giving them the outcome they desire.

Once we determine the goals of our Receiver based on their answers, we then may need to adjust the quantity of oils used and we may even decide to change which oils will be used.

The questions I suggest may seem formal–more appropriate for the Receivers you see within your Raindrop Practice–but the concepts behind the questions should still be considered if you are offering Raindrop to your best friend, mom, or kids.

The Questions to Ask

When I first started doing Raindrops, I did not change the oils or amount used; I stuck with The Basic Recipe because that was what I was taught. Many of the people who I gave Raindrops to enjoyed it, but there were some who detoxed more than expected. They were shocked, and I was surprised as well. Even though they enjoyed the experience of receiving a Raindrop, they did not like how they felt afterwards. If I had asked them the questions I am going to share with you, then I could have tailored the Raindrop to fit their situation. Most likely, they would have experienced a gentle detox versus an unexpected and unwanted grand detox that kept them at home for a few days.

During the fifteen years that I've been offering Raindrop Technique Massage as a Massage Therapist and teaching Raindrop as a CARE (Center for Aromatherapy Research and Education, Inc.) Instructor, I have noticed an increase in allergies, pharmaceutical use, and toxin load. I love how Raindrop supports us in so many ways, but because of the increase of ill health, I feel it is important to adapt our Raindrops to fit our Receivers. I want my Receiver to detox slowly, and have a pleasant and educational experience. A little discomfort, whether physical, emotional, or spiritual, is a good thing, because with this type of discomfort comes increased health and spiritual growth. However, if there is too much discomfort without support from you, they may not want to return again for more Raindrop sessions. If they detox too fast, like some of my first clients did, without education on or planning for the detox, they will not come back and the miracles of Raindrop will be lost to them.

This is what prompted me to start changing the amount of oil used. We know that "more is not always better" and that "less is more" when it comes to essential oil use, so why can't we apply that same concept to Raindrop?

I started asking questions too. I have a health history form that I use in my massage practice, but I realized it doesn't answer the questions I need for a Raindrop session. I wanted to get a better understanding of what their toxic load might be like. I also took time to explain my reasoning behind asking these questions. When I explained that their answers revealed whether they could be holding on to toxins, this made my clients think about their health in a new way.

In my head, I categorized their answers as colored flags. I'm going to use these flag colors here to help us discuss what considerations we should take for each kind of "flag."

We have Red Flag, Yellow Flag, and Green Flag answers.

Red Flags let me know that this person is most likely toxic and I need to adjust the amount of Essential Oils used so they don't have more of a detoxing experience than they signed up for.

Yellow Flags tell me that I most likely will need to pull back a bit on the amount of essential oils used.

Green Flags give me the idea that I do not have to worry about this person becoming overly detoxed, and I probably don't have to reduce the amount of essential oil being used.

Eight Questions + Eight Flags = A Tailored Raindrop

The following eight questions are what I normally ask my Raindrop Receivers, especially if they are a new client. These simple questions will help you learn about their goals for their session with you, which can assist in tailoring their Raindrop. You'll also get an indication of their toxic load. Make sure you explain the "why" behind the toxic questions.

First question:

"What are your goals in receiving this Raindrop today?"

This first question not only plays a huge role in how we can tailor our Raindrop to that person, but it gives intention for both Receiver and Giver. This question gets the Receiver involved with their Raindrop experience and outcome.

Common responses:

Just relaxation

To reduce back pain

Immune support

To detox

I don't know, my sister told me to do it

To release some negative emotions

Second Question:

"What do you do during the day? What is your job?"

This lets us know how many toxins they are routinely exposed to without having to ask them directly. After they tell you what they do, I'm sure they will share more with you once you explain: "I always ask this question just so I can get an idea of how many toxins or chemicals you are exposed to daily. How many toxins do you think you are exposed to regularly?"

Possible Answers:
- Nail tech

    Librarian

🚩 Naturopath

Third Question:

"How often do you eat fast food/processed foods?"

This question also gives us an idea of their possible toxic load.

Possible Answers:

🚩 For Lunch I always grab fast food and a soda.

🚩 Once a week I'll grab something for dinner with the kids.

🚩 I make all my meals at home using only organic ingredients.

Fourth Question

"How often do you have a bowel movement?"

Don't be uncomfortable with this question - it is SO important! You need to know how well their digestive system is functioning. When the phenols do their detoxing job and your Receivers' exits are not moving, where are those toxins going to go? If they have a backup in their large intestines and they are not having regular bowel movements, then those toxins are going to have to find another exit route. This person has a greater chance of getting a rash from their detox since their colon is backed up and moving slow.

Possible Answers:

🚩 Well… I go about once a week.

🚩 I usually go once a day but lately it's been about a few times a week.

🚩 I go one or two times a day.

Fifth Question:

"How much water do you drink a day on average?"

This question goes along with Question Four. If they are not cleansing their body with water, that lets us know that they are holding on to toxins.

Possible Answers:

⚑ I hate water, I drink diet soda and energy drinks.

   I am trying to drink more water. About two to three 8 ounce bottles a day. In the morning I have two cups of coffee.

⚑ I am making it a point to drink about six to eight 8 ounce bottles of water a day.

Sixth Question:

"Tell me about your essential oil use? How long have you been using them and how do you use them?"

If someone is new to using essential oils, then we will want to use less with them. We don't know how their body responds to essential oils yet, and they may be holding on to more toxins, too. Someone who has been using essential oils for years is more familiar with how their body responds and is probably more familiar to detoxing.

Possible Answers:

⚑ I don't use oils, my sister does. She loves them and told me I needed a Raindrop.

   I just started using them a month ago. I diffuse them everyday and just started putting oregano on my feet everyday since the flu is going around. I do love those oils.

⚑ I've been using oils for over six years. I diffuse, put them on my feet, and take them in a capsule now and then in the wintertime.

Seventh Question:

"Have you had Raindrop before?"

If someone has not experienced Raindrop before, then we don't know what their response will be to all of those different oils. If they have not had a Raindrop with *you* then you still don't know what their response will be. This first session is a time for you to learn more about this Receiver. Their responses to these questions and to the Raindrop done with you will give you information on how you should proceed for the next Raindrop.

Possible Answers:

- No.
- Yes.

Eighth Question

"Do you have any allergies to citrus, wheat, coconut, or nuts?"

I have a client who is allergic to citrus. That means I can't use Joy™ or Peace 'n Calming® on her. To be safe, I stick with the singles with her and do not use blends.

Valor® has a base oil of Caprylic/capric triglyceride. This is a rather safe base oil for topical use. It's usually made from combining coconut oil with glycerin. Only people who are highly allergic to coconut have a problem with this base oil.

Aroma Ease has Fractionated Cocos nucifera (Coconut) oil as the first ingredient. It also contains Triticum vulgare (Wheat) germ oil, Prunus amygdalus dulcis (Sweet almond) oil.

If your Receiver states that they have an allergy to a specific essential oil, we'll discuss how to approach choosing another essential oil for them in Chapter Four.

Here is a quick review of the Eight Questions:

1. What are your goals with receiving this Raindrop today?
2. What do you do during the day? What is your job?
3. How often do you eat fast food?
4. How often do you have a bowel movement?
5. How much water do you drink a day on average?
6. Tell me about your essential oil use? How long have you been using them and how do you use them?
7. Have you had a Raindrop before?
8. Do you have any allergies to citrus, wheat, coconut, or nuts?

Tailoring Raindrop

Now let's take a look at the answers to these eight questions with a few hypothetical clients. We'll discuss how we could tailor the oil amount and choices for each one.

Person #1

Q1: 🚩 Just relaxation.

Q2: 🚩 Nail tech.

Q3: 🚩 For lunch I always grab fast food with a soda.

Q4: ⚑ I usually go once a day but lately it has been about a few times a week.

Q5: ⚑ I am trying to drink more water, about two to three 8 oz bottles a day. In the morning I have two cups of coffee.

Q6: 🚩 I don't use oils, my sister does. She loves them and told me I needed a Raindrop.

Q7: 🚩 No, I haven't had a Raindrop before.

Q8: ⚑ No, I don't have any allergies.

Now you know that this nail tech is most likely carrying a pretty heavy toxic load due to her profession. To add to her toxicity, she eats out a lot and her bowels are not moving well. She doesn't have experience with essential oils or Raindrop, and her goal is simply relaxation, not for a detox. She has not been prepared for detoxing. This is someone we will need to reduce the amount of oils used in their Raindrop for sure! If she was on my table, I would switch out some oils to support relaxation instead of detoxing, and greatly reduce the amount of oils used.

Person #2

Q1: 🚩 To support my respiratory system.

Q2: 🚩 Librarian.

Q3: 🚩 I make all my meals at home using only organic ingredients.

Q4: 🚩 I go one or two times a day.

Q5: 🚩 I am trying to drink more water. About two to three 8 oz bottles a day. In the morning I have two cups of coffee.

Q6: 🚩 I just started using them a month ago. I diffuse them all day and just recently started putting oils on my feet daily. I do love those oils.

Q7: 🚩 No, I haven't had a Raindrop before.

Q8: 🚩 I am allergic to gluten.

This librarian is making some great health choices. He eats organically and makes his meals at home which will reduce his toxic load. He's drinking his water and he's having regular bowel movements which means he is ridding himself of many toxins he may be exposed to. He is fairly new to essential oils, but is responding well to them. With someone like this, we would reduce the amount of oils used since he never had a Raindrop before. I would create a "system supporting Raindrop" to offer support to his respiratory system. Since he does have a gluten allergy, I would not use AromaEase and would replace it with Safflower oil (or another simple base oil).

Person #3

Q1: 🚩 To release negative emotions.

Q2: 🚩 Naturopath.

Q3: 🚩 I make all my meals at home using only organic ingredients.

Q4: 🚩 I go one or two times a day.

Q5: 🚩 I am trying to drink more water. About six to eight 8 oz bottles a day. In the morning I have tea.

Q6: 🚩 I've been using oils for over six years. I diffuse and apply topically daily.

Q7: 🚩 No, I haven't had a Raindrop before.

Q8: 🚩 No, I don't have allergies.

Even though this Naturopath is eating a healthy diet, drinking her water, and has been using oils for a long time, I'd still reduce the amount of oils used simply because she has never had a Raindrop before. Neither one of us knows what her response will be to all of the various essential oils. She also is looking for an emotional release, so that lets me know that a big physical detox is not the goal, and that we should be focused on emotions. We will spend time doing some work prior to the Raindrop to create a unique "Emotional Releasing Raindrop" for her.

Person #4

Q1: 🚩 Detox.

Q2: 🚩 Massage therapist.

Q3: 🚩 Twice a month I'll grab something for dinner with the kids.

Q4: 🚩 I go one or two times a day.

Q5: 🚩 I am trying to drink more water. About two to three 8 oz bottles a day. In the morning I have two cups of coffee.

Q6: 🚩 I've been using oils for over five years. I diffuse, put them on my feet and take them in a capsule in the wintertime.

Q7: 🚩 Yes, with you many times!

Q8: 🚩 No, I don't have allergies.

This massage therapist is a friend of mine. I know her well and we've been trading Raindrops for a long time now. She is pretty healthy and drinks her water. She is a big Oiler and gets a Raindrop from me monthly. Her goal is detoxing. She scheduled this appointment with me on a Saturday so she'll have Sunday and Monday–her days off–to relax. I would feel comfortable using the full amount of oils on her and may add some oils in for liver and lymph support to assist in the detoxing.

When You Do the Math

Three drops per foot X eight oils X two feet = forty-eight drops

Four drops on the back X eight oils = thirty-two drops

For a total of eighty drops of essential oil.

That really is quite a lot of essential oils for someone who is new to Raindrop, or totally new to essential oils. Using this amount of oil on someone who is holding on to a lot of toxins will typically lead to a heavy detox. Tailoring the amount of essential oils being used is the most common way to adapt your Raindrop.

Adapting For Detoxing

How do we adapt The Basic Recipe to make sure someone does not detox too much? Here are some ideas:

Apply base oil on the spine before you add any essential oils. This slows down the absorption of the oils, especially the first few which are the "phenolic" cleansing oils.

Simply reduce the number of drops used in Raindrop. A common suggestion is three drops per foot for the Foot VitaFlex and four to six drops on the back for each oil.

You can always reduce the number of drops to one per foot and one on the back. That will bring it to twenty-four drops. That is way more appropriate for someone who is healthy, new to oils, and not indicating that they are holding onto a lot of toxins.

Lorrie Papach, Certified Raindrop Technique Specialist (CRTS), Licensed Spiritual Healer (LSH), shared a great tip on how to reduce detoxing from Raindrop to avoid taking the detox too far. She said, "I dilute with 50% grape seed so there are likely no allergies. I have an extra set of bottles and just fill them half and half, since I learned it doesn't lessen the effectiveness but lessens rapid detox. It is what I prefer."

When I have a Receiver with a lot of red flags, that lets me know there is a good chance they are holding on to many toxins and/or they may be new to essential oils. Based on this information, I may make the decision to reduce the amount of oils used by doing a half of a Raindrop.

There are a few options to doing a Half Raindrop. One way is to do just the Spinal VitaFlex points on their feet with the essential oils and then transition into another wellness technique I offer. Another option I often use is to either totally skip the foot VitaFlex or do the spinal points on the feet without any essential oils. Then continuing the Raindrop session by only applying the essential oils to their back, of course using all the techniques typically used in Raindrop. Doing half of a Raindrop is one simple way to reduce the number of essential oils you apply to your Receiver while still offering them the experience and support they are looking for.

Let's check out the characteristics of the oils again to give us a better idea of which oils are the "heavy cleaners" of the group.

Oil	P, M or S
Valor	Monoterpenes & Sesquiterpenes
Oregano	Phenols
Thyme	Phenols
Basil	Phenols
Wintergreen	Phenols
Marjoram	Monoterpenes
Cypress	Monoterpenes & Sesquiterpenes
Peppermint	Phenols

You can see that five of the oils are the heavy cleaners. These oils have a high concentration of phenols. Now, we do want to do *some* cleaning for sure–that is one of the benefits of Raindrop. We want to add some cleaners, but we certainly want to pull back on the amount of high-phenol oils used with someone whose responses had a lot of "red flag" answers.

Practical Examples

Remember our Receiver scenarios? Their responses helped us learn more about their toxic load, their goals, and their past oil exposure. Now let's see how we may adapt their Raindrop to give us a better chance of achieving their goals. Remember, all of these are suggestions and possibilities to give you different choices and ideas on how to adapt the Raindrop for individual Receivers. You can use one, two, or all three of the ideas.

<u>Person #1</u>

The Nail Tech who is totally new to oils, has a toxic load, and her bowel movements are sluggish. Here are some possible adaptations to make for her:

Do a Half of a Raindrop

-VitaFlex on the feet only with one drop of each oil per foot, or…

-Raindrop on the back with one drop of each oil

-Add in other relaxing modalities that you offer to fit the session time.

Dilute

-This is a perfect person to use the 50/50 dilution method as Lorrie recommends. Even with dilution, I would still reduce the number of oils to one to two drops of each oil on the feet and one drop of each oil on the back.

-This will allow you to give a full Raindrop experience.

Tailor it!

This Receiver was looking for relaxation, so perhaps I can remove the oregano and thyme (heavy cleaners) and jump right to wintergreen, basil, and marjoram which have some phenols, too, but definitely not as much. She'll get some cleaning, but not an overload, and we'll add in oils for relaxation, which is her main goal. I may put a Raindrop together that contains these oils: basil, marjoram, Peace & Calming® Blend, lavender, cypress, Valor®, and peppermint.

<u>Person #2</u>

The Librarian who eats organic foods, drinks lots of water, and has one to two bowel movements a day. I don't think he has a large toxic load, but he is new to oils and Raindrop, so I'm going to go slow and see how he responds.

Reduce the Amount of Oils Used

    VitaFlex on the feet:

    -Use all the oils in The Basic Recipe

    -One drop per foot

    Oils on the back:

    -Apply base oil first to slow down the absorption

    -Use one to two drops of oils in The Basic Recipe

Dilute

This is a perfect person to use the 50/50 dilution method as Lorrie recommends. Use one to two drops on the feet, and two to four drops on the back.

Tailor It!

Create a unique Raindrop using the System Supporting Raindrop (found in Chapter Four).

Person #3

This is our organic Naturopath who has been using oils for years, has regular bowel movements, and is making an effort to drink eight glasses of 8 oz of water a day.

Basic Amount of Oils Used

    VitaFlex on the feet:

    -Use all the oils

    -Two to three drops per foot

    On the back:

    -Use two to three drops of oils in The Basic Recipe

Dilute

This is a perfect person to use the 50/50 dilution method on. Diluting the essential oils allows you to use more drops during their session while still reducing the total amount of essential oils they are exposed to.

Tailor it!

We will do research before her Raindrop to plan which oils to include to help her reach her emotional release goal.

We may choose to do an "Emotional Release Raindrop" as discussed in Chapter Five.

Person #4

This is our Massage Therapist who doesn't have a purely organic lifestyle, but she drinks her water and has a lot of experience with Raindrop. I've done many Raindrops on her, so I'm comfortable with how she responds, as is she. Her focus for this Raindrop is detoxing and she has put aside time to relax if she does experience a strong detox reaction (such as feeling extremely tired, having an upset stomach, extra bowel movements, headache, or a skin rash).

Basic Amount of Oils Used

VitaFlex on the feet:

-Use all the oils

-Two to three drops per foot

On the back:

-Use three to four drops of the oils in The Basic Recipe.

Tailor it!

Add additional oils to support the liver, colon, and/or lymphatic system, or do a System Supporting Raindrop.

Follow up!

It is important that your Receiver drinks plenty of water after a Raindrop to help remove the toxins that have just been cleaned away. Give them water right away and educate them about the possible side effects of detoxing they may experience.

Sometimes we get so focused on the detoxing possibilities that it is easy to forget to discuss the benefits of Raindrop of which there are many! Raindrop can relax your muscles, leave you feeling grounded, help you feel mentally and physically connected, help you sleep better, give you immunity support, reduce back and neck pain, provide emotional release, and more. Make sure you mention these positive aspects alongside detox indicators. We want people to focus on all the good things that Raindrop can do for them.

Make sure you check in with them the next day. Ask how they are feeling, if they are drinking their water, and if they experienced any other changes. Getting their feedback on how they responded will help you determine the amount of essential oils you'll use for their next Raindrop.

If they are having any issues or struggles with detoxing, you can support them and remind them that this cleanse will be worthwhile. When those toxins are eliminated (and if we don't add them back in) then they are gone for good! Cleansing is a good thing! It may be helpful to remind them of the benefits this cleanse will bring to them and their bodies.

Talking with your Receiver and learning about how they felt after their first Raindrop session will be the indicator of how you proceed with their next session. Did they detox a lot? If that is the case, then you know you still need to reduce the amount of oils you use for the following appointment. If they detoxed just a little bit, and they were comfortable with that level of detox, then stay with that amount of oils for the next few sessions. Asking questions about how long they detoxed, getting an idea of how they felt about the detox, and learning about the other changes they noticed from their Raindrop will be used to decide what your next session will be like. Your role is to be an observer during the session, immediately after and the day after the Raindrop.

A Raindropper's Promise: "Thou Shall Not Skimp on Cypress or Valor®"

The two oils in The Basic Recipe that you never want to reduce for any Receiver are Valor® (or another balancing oil) and cypress. There are a few reasons for that.

Valor® and cypress don't contain many phenols so they will not add to the detoxing that Raindrop provides. In other words, you don't need to worry about them contributing to overly detoxing Receivers.

Valor® is a balancing oil. It supports the Receiver by balancing their energy and emotions. We all need that, don't we? When Valor® is used towards the end of Raindrop it is meant to help the Receiver hold any changes that they have experienced. I see Valor® as the glue to Raindrop.

As noted previously, Valor® has a base oil of caprylic/capric triglyceride. If someone is highly allergic to coconut, then a replacement oil such as frankincense, Believe® blend, or Transformation® can be used to offer balance to the Receiver's energy and emotion.

Cypress is mainly monoterpenes and sesquiterpenes. This essential oil supports the circulatory system, including the venous system and the lymphatic system.

I get very excited about the lymph system because it helps to remove toxins, large protein molecules, viruses, and bacteria from our body. We always want this system to be supported and working well, but we want it to be working *very* well if someone will be detoxing. This is the system that will be "taking out the trash" that those phenol molecules are kicking up. Using cypress essential oil, staying hydrated, and walking are the three best ways to support the lymph system.

CHAPTER THREE
Adding Other Oils

When I think about adding other oils into a Raindrop, I hear a line in my head from one of my daughter's favorite movies. The teen heroine of the movie loves baking, and while she is visiting her extended family in Paris, France, she learns the secret of "Je ne sais quoi," which in French means "I don't know." In a recipe, it is the special ingredient that is used to make the recipe unique. This "je ne sais quoi" will not be the same each time the recipe is used. The same is true for your Raindrops.

Why Would You Want to Add Other Oils to Raindrop?

We may add other oils if the Receiver has a specific goal that can be addressed with a particular oil. This could be an emotional goal (to give clarity, bring joy, or to be more present), or a physical goal (to support the digestive system, respiratory system, or the brain). Perhaps your Receiver would like to investigate the possible emotional causes of their physical ailment. This is when you can do some investigation together and create their "Emotional Releasing Raindrop." You may also get a nudge or feeling that a certain oil would complement the Raindrop and have greater support for your Receiver.

Which Oil and When?

There are a few ways you can determine which oil or oils to add:

1. *After the Trio*

In CARE Training, we teach that you can add additional oils to support our client after the three oils we refer to as the "Trio" (basil, wintergreen, and marjoram) are applied.

2. *"Why are you receiving this Raindrop Today?"*

If you are asking the eight questions I suggested in Chapter Two, the first question, "Why are you receiving this Raindrop Today?" can often lead you right to the answer of which oils to add. If someone is looking for respiratory support, then you can add an oil that supports the respiratory system such as Eucalyptus globulus, Raven™, or R.C.™ Blend. If someone is looking for digestive support, then perhaps adding fennel or DiGize Blend would be appropriate.

If you don't know which oil will support the Receiver in their Raindrop goal, then take a look in your *Essential Oils Desk Reference*. That will offer you many choices for your Receiver's goal.

Perhaps they need emotional support. Let's remember our Nail Tech in the examples who was looking for relaxation. What are some oils that would support her goal? Lavender, frankincense, or Stress Away Blend come to mind for me, what about you?

Maybe the goal is a spiritual one, perhaps a release of a negative emotion that is holding them back. You may have a system planned out for digging through emotions and choosing a supporting oil. If you don't, then the "Emotional Release Raindrop" protocol may give you some ideas.

3. *They Will Tell You*

Many of my clients who are familiar with essential oils know right away what they want added. Some even bring their own oils with them.

4. *Through Observation*

Sometimes the Receiver may not know what would support them, or exactly what support they are looking for. Instead they may tell you their story. Listen to their words and observe their posture and facial expressions. Paying attention to body language can provide you with a lot of information. You may hear in your head or heart, or feel in your body the oils that would be a support for them.

One client who came to see me for Raindrop shared that her mom had passed away six months ago and she felt that her heart was still heavy. The oils I pulled out of my kit to include in her Raindrop were Joy™ Blend, Gentle Baby™ Blend, and frankincense.

When I'm choosing an oil for emotional support, I usually don't tell the receiver which oil I'm adding to the technique or that I'm even adding oils. I want their brain to be able to relax instead of trying to think about why a particular oil was or was not chosen. At the end of the session, when they are dressed and drinking their water, I will share which oils I used if they should ask. Often they will say, "that was just the right oil," or "that was what I needed, thank you."

A few years ago, I had one client who oozed sadness. Her energy was low, her speech was slow, and her posture was slouched. She made Eeyore, the Winnie the Pooh character, look like the life of the party. She was driving through town and wanted a Raindrop. She told me she had received a Raindrop before and it had helped her back. When I asked what her goal was in receiving this Raindrop, she didn't quite have an answer, but told me she was on this road trip to help her family.

I pulled out three oils for her to smell and see which one she was attracted to. Here are her replies to the scent of each oil:

Frankincense - "It smells ok."

Live My Passion® Blend - "It's not bad."

Joy™ Blend - "This oil does not smell at all."

You know which oil I chose, right? It was Joy™ Blend!

When she finished her Raindrop session with me, she was walking upright, there was a little twinkle in her eye again, and she said she felt ready to continue her trip. I gave her a call the following day to check in, and she told me all about the many sad and stressful events that were going on with her family in the past few months. She told me that since her Raindrop, she felt lighter and better.

Listen to the voice

When I first started giving Raindrops, I would be in the middle of a session and I would have an oil name pop into my head. At first I discounted that voice and told myself, "Who am I to determine what they need?" It kept on happening, and one time at the end of the session, I decided to mention the oil that came to my mind to the Receiver. It turned out that it would have been the perfect oil to add, and she would have benefited from the support it offered.

After that, I started adding the oils that popped into my head. Each time I mentioned the oil I added, my Receiver would tell me a personal story about what was going on with them… it turned out to be just the right oil to add!

It took me a while to gain the confidence to listen to the voice in my head. I'm sure God was shaking his head each time I discounted that voice. I was a slow learner. Please let my experience shorten your learning time! If you are giving a Raindrop and in your head, heart, or stomach you feel the need to add a particular oil, listen to that feeling!

There is not one single way to choose an additional oil for your Receiver. The best advice I have for you is to listen to your Receiver and be observant of what is behind their words. Then listen to your own intuition, gut, voice, or heart. This approach will never lead you wrong!

CHAPTER FOUR
Replacing an Oil

When you are cooking, there are three reasons to replace the ingredients called for in the recipe:
1. Sometimes you need to replace ingredients because you are missing an ingredient. I often do this when I don't have the milk called for in a muffin recipe. Instead, I'll use yogurt.
2. Another time you may swap out an ingredient is because of an allergy, like using almond milk instead of dairy milk.
3. You may also need to replace ingredients to tailor your meal for a specific person's taste buds.

The same is true for swapping out oils when it comes to Raindrops. Let's talk about what to do with each case!

When You are Missing an Oil

Sometimes you may not have all the essential oils in The Basic Recipe because you ran out of the oil or it is out of stock. There have been a few instances in my Raindrop career where Young Living was out of a few of the Raindrop oils. If I remember correctly, we were out of wintergreen at one point, cypress another time, and Valor® for a (heartbreakingly) long period of time. This can happen when working with plants and when you are using essential oils from a company that will not sell you something that is below their strict requirements.

This is not a time to panic and stop doing Raindrops, but is a time to get creative and look at the possibilities of using other essential oils that have similar characteristics.

Young Living recently expanded into South Africa in September of 2019. They were not able to provide all of the oils immediately for distributors to purchase in South Africa.

One of the CARE Instructors reached out to the other instructors with a list of the oils available in South Africa, and asked for some advice: "We can't get oregano and basil yet. What oils would you use to replace oregano and basil for Raindrop?"

It was interesting to see the different ways that people approached this same question. I feel that people solve this kind of problem based on their personalities. Some people are "book" people and others are "gut" people. Book people like to research and have solid information to help them make a decision. For them to feel comfortable with their decision, they need evidence pulled from a book, chart, graph, or article to back them up. Gut people don't necessarily need to find the information in a book, but are comfortable with going by their intuition or past experience.

Either way of approaching which oil to use is fine, and both often lead to the same solution. You can choose which way you are comfortable with. Both work, so no worries!

When There is an Allergy

The same is true for someone who says they have an allergy to an oil. When I first started using essential oils I was taught that you can't have an allergy to pure essential oils because true essential oils don't contain protein molecules. You can read all about allergies and protein molecules in the *Chemistry of Essential Oils* by Dr. David Stewart (Chapter 12, "Allergies").

As the years have passed and I've worked with more and more people, I have seen some unusual responses to essential oils. Whether they come from allergies, emotional responses, or detoxing, I'm not sure. One thing I am sure of is if someone tells me they are allergic to an oil, whether it is peppermint, wintergreen, or another oil, I will not argue with them. I'll inform them that it is protein molecules that we are allergic to and pure essential oils do not contain proteins. I'll also share that the food additives or scents in candles are man-made molecules that we are allergic to, and that allergies do not stem from the natural plant molecules we find in essential oils. Then I leave it in their hands. If they still are adamant that they are allergic to that oil, then I will remove it from the Raindrop they will be receiving and replace it with another oil that has a similar characteristic.

We know that intention and thought has a great deal to do with the outcome of our oils and Raindrop. I don't want my Receiver to experience their Raindrop with a fear that there may be a chance they could have an allergic reaction to an oil being used. We don't want fear or worry to have a place in their Raindrop experience.

How to Choose a Replacement

If you are choosing a replacement oil for one that is out of stock or for an allergy, you can go about it the same way.

Let's use South Africa as an example. Here is a list of oils that you could purchase from Young Living if you lived in South Africa in September 2019. If you notice, there are two important Raindrop oils that are not on the list: oregano and basil.

Single Oils

1. Bergamot – 5ml
2. Cypress – 5ml
3. Eucalyptus Globulus – 5ml
4. Eucalyptus Radiata – 5ml
5. Frankincense – 5ml & 15ml
6. Geranium – 5ml
7. Grapefruit – 5ml & 15ml
8. Lavender – 5ml & 15ml
9. Lemon – 5ml & 15ml
10. Lemongrass – 5ml & 15ml
11. Myrrh – 5ml
12. Orange – 5ml & 15ml
13. Patchouli – 5ml
14. Cedarwood – 15ml
15. Citronella – 5ml
16. Clary Sage – 5ml
17. Copaiba – 5ml
18. Helichrysum – 5ml
19. Peppermint 5ml & 15ml
20. Rose – 5ml
21. Sacred Frankincense – 5ml
22. Spearmint – 5ml
23. Tea Tree – 5ml & 15ml
24. Wintergreen – 5ml
25. Ylang Ylang – 5ml
26. Vetiver – 5ml

Oil Blends

27. Christmas Spirit – 5ml
28. Citrus Fresh – 5ml & 15ml
29. Joy – 5ml
30. 12-month ER Loyalty Blend – 5ml
31. Melrose – 5ml
32. Peace & Calming – 5ml & 15ml
33. Purification – 5ml & 15ml
34. RC – 5ml & 15ml
35. Thieves – 5ml & 15ml
36. Raven – 5ml
37. Valor – 5ml & 15ml
38. White Angelica – 5ml
39. YL Haven (Stress Away) – 5ml & 15ml

There are three ways that someone could approach choosing a replacement oil:
1. Using Chemistry
2. Using an Essential Oil Reference Book
3. Using the Oil's Characteristics

Let's talk about these in further detail. I will walk you through the steps involved with each option.

1. Using Chemistry
- Using *The Chemistry of Essential Oils*, look on page 498 to find the scientific name of oregano.
- Now turn to page 541 to look at Origanum compactum. We can see that oregano has 60% to 80% of phenols. We want to find an oil that has about that same amount.
- On page 571 there is a list of oils that have a high percentage of phenols. Choose an oil in your possession that has a similar amount of phenols.
- Some of the oils that have a high percentage of phenols are clove, fennel, and basil. You could choose from these to replace oregano.

The upside to finding a replacement oil this way is how quickly you can find an alternative, and that it gives you a few possible oils to choose from. The downside to choosing this way is that oils that have a large amount of the same constituent, like phenols, don't always support our bodies in the same way.

2. Using The Essential Oil Desk Reference (EODR) 4th Edition
- Let's take a look at how oregano can support us. You can find that on page 85 in the EODR. Under the "Medical Properties" section, you'll see that oregano can support us in many ways. This gives us the opportunity to tailor your Raindrop a bit. Is the Receiver looking for more immune support (antiviral and antibacterial properties) or perhaps more muscular support (anti-inflammatory properties)?
- Using the "Personal Usage Reference" section, look up what your Receiver is trying to prevent or support. We'll say they want to support their immune system so they don't get the cold that has been going around the office. Look up "Colds" on page 373.

- You'll find some oils that are recommended for preventing colds. Choose one that you have.

3. Using the Oil's Characteristics
    - Each oil used in the Raindrop Technique is going to support the body in a different way since they each target a different system. One way to find a suitable replacement is to look at an oil's characteristics. For example, oregano is a "cleaner" and supports the immune system.
    - The chart below gives you a quick look at which system each oil supports. We simply need to find an oil that has similar characteristics. You may know right away, or you may need to look in your reference guide for suggestions.

Looking at our original example about the essential oils that were available in South Africa, which oil or blend would you use for oregano?

At some time, you may need to find replacements for other oils not related to the Raindrop Technique. Now you have a path to a solution!

Tailor your Raindrop to Fit That Person's Specific Needs

One time, I invited dinner guests over and had planned to make a Chinese meal. I had rice, shrimp, carrots, onions, garlic, cashews, and soy sauce ready to whip up the dish.

Before dinner was cooked, we were chatting and nibbling on appetizers. My friend told me about how she had been on vacation and was sick for days! She had food poisoning after going to a Chinese restaurant and she said, "I was *so* sick, I don't think I will ever eat Chinese food again!"

Well, thankfully I didn't choke on my appetizer. I excused myself and slipped back into the kitchen to look at my ingredients. After contemplating my ingredients for a few minutes, I created a new meal plan. I replaced the cashews with cherry tomatoes and switched the soy sauce with fresh oregano and olive oil. My Chinese stir fry was transformed into an Italian risotto, which I was so glad to hear was just what my dinner guest had "been craving!"

We can do the same "ingredient swap" with our essential oils that are in The Basic Recipe to create a Raindrop that will totally support the Receiver's needs.

An example of this oil ingredient swap is found in *Essential Oils Integrative Medical Guide*, on page 228. This wheel that Gary Young created gives us a wonderful, quick guide to how we can tailor our Raindrops to support a very specific need of the Receiver.

I asked for permission to use a copy of that wheel in this resource guide, but I was told I could not, so instead I'll describe it. The center of the wheel has three oils that are the "hub" of Raindrop: Valor®, oregano, and thyme. First you need to balance with Valor®, then clean with oregano and thyme.

When following The Basic Recipe, the next oils used are the Trio: basil, wintergreen and marjoram. The wheel shows us that we can replace the Trio with two to four oils that support a certain body system. If you find that wheel, don't feel like you need to use all of the oils suggested. Use two to four of the oils that you have.

You may have noticed that you will not find cypress in the wheel, but I feel that this oil is a must to add to any Raindrop recipe. If you are "cleaning" with oregano, thyme, and other phenolic oils, you always want to support the lymphatic system with cypress. So please, please, please, always add that to your tailored recipe.

I also suggest you finish with the Balancing blend, which is often Valor®. The effect of this oil is to help the body to hold changes, especially emotional and spinal alignments.

What if you don't have the oils suggested in the wheel? What if you are looking to support your Receiver in a different way than suggested on the wheel? Either way, simply search an essential oil reference guide for the oils that are suggested for that goal and use two to four of the suggested oils.

How cool is this? This concept now opens you up to countless Raindrop recipes that are specific to your Receiver and their current situation.

To help you see or plan what I call a "System Supporting Raindrop," I created the cart for you on the following page.

Detoxing Considerations Still Apply

Remember, all the detoxing thoughts and advice in Chapter Two still apply on these Tailored Raindrop Recipes, too. You can still give a very targeted Raindrop and reduce the oils that you use. Perhaps you only do the Raindrop on the back and omit the feet. Again, the same thoughts apply. Ask questions and follow your intuition on the amount of oils used.

I have also included in the "Essential Oil Ideas" some suggestions of which oils to use to support a specific system of the body. These are not the only oil choices, but a few of my favorite ones. Using a reference guide will give you more ideas and choices.

System Supporting Raindrop

Step 1: Start with balancing.
Step 2: Foot VitaFlex the spinal points on the feet.

	Step 3 Apply "Cleaners"	Step 4 Support a System	Step 5 Support Lymphatic System	Step 6 Balance & Finish
Oil	Oregano Thyme	Choose one, two or three oils or blends to support a system or goal.	Cypress	Valor®/ Balancing Oil & Peppermint
Technique	Apply and feather these as typically done in Raindrop.	See "Suggested Oils" Chart for ideas.	Use the following techniques after applying cypress. • Thumb VitaFlex • Finger Straddle • Stretch & Rock • Apply base oil • Palm Slide	Apply each oil with Feathering and Arched Feather Strokes. Finish with moist heat pack.

(Oil order and techniques follow CARE Raindrop instruction).

Essential Oil Ideas

Digestive System	Endocine System	Immune Support	Lymphatic System
Dill Fennel Ginger	Nutmeg Bergamot Clary Sage	Clove Rosemary Lemon Myrtle	Ginger Juniper Grapefruit

Muscular System	Relaxation	Respiratory System	Skeletal System
Clove Lavender Black Pepper	Lavender Tangerine Chamomile	Pine Myrtle Eucalyptus glob	Pine Clove Lemongrass

CHAPTER FIVE
An Emotional Release Raindrop

~ For Spiritual Healers ~

You are in such a unique field, and what I firmly believe to be a quickly growing field. I think you are meant for this time in history and I am excited for you.

This is a Raindrop tip that I've saved just for you, because I knew you would appreciate it.

As an LCCI, I teach the five hour "Emotional Release with Essential Oil" class in CARE Intensives. I love Emotional Release, but as I tell students in my class, the most practical part of this class is learning how to use the books to work on your own emotional baggage (*Heal Your Body*, by Louise Hay, *Releasing Emotional Patterns with Essential Oils* by Carolyn Mein, D.C., and *Feelings Buried Alive Never Die* by Karol Truman). Once you get comfortable using the three books, then you can help others walk through the process.

When we get to the facilitated Emotional Release section of class, we usually have an hour and half left of the Intensive, certainly not enough time for a fully facilitated Emotional Release session that you would hold with a client. I always share that this part of the class is just to give you a "taste" of what a facilitated Emotional Release is like. A real session usually takes around three hours, one hour for each phase (opening, clearing, and reprogramming). Each time I teach this CARE class, I have students contact me later asking for a facilitated emotional release for themselves.

As a spiritual healer, many of my Emotional Release clients are moms dealing with emotional issues, and looking for help to release negative baggage. I want to help them, but it can be difficult for both of us to free up three hours to fit in an Emotional Release session. So instead, I cooked up another Raindrop recipe that I now refer to as an "Emotional Release Raindrop."

An Emotional Release Raindrop can be completed in one and a half hours, from start to finish. The amount of oils used for this Raindrop is much less than what is applied in a facilitated Emotional Release as taught in a CARE Emotional Release class. I find that the Receiver does not release on the table, but instead they release when they are alone in a private place.

My clients have told me they experienced the release while they were driving home, in the shower, or through a dream that night which is related to the issue we focused on during their session. All of these Receivers felt better, lighter, happier, and saw a positive change in their spouse, kids, themselves, etc., which they felt was due to their release.

I have to say that I love this way of supporting Receivers emotionally with essential oils and Raindrop.

An Emotional Release Raindrop

To use an Emotional Release Raindrop, we are going to use a similar pattern as the "System Supporting Raindrop," but to find out which oils to add we are going to do some book work with our Receiver first.

Books to use with your Receiver to do research include:
- *Releasing Emotional Patterns with Essential Oils*, by Carolyn Mein, D.C.
- *Heal Your Body*, by Louise Hay
- *The Pathway to Emotional Healing*, by Jen McCraw
- *Feelings Buried Alive Never Die,* by Karol Truman

If your Receiver knows which emotion they are dealing with, then you can start with *Releasing Emotional Patterns with Essential Oils,* or *The Pathway*. If your Receiver is dealing with a physical issue of which they would like to explore the emotional cause, then you are going to start with *Heal Your Body*, or *The Pathway,* or *Feelings Buried Alive Never Die.*

During the first twenty to thirty minutes of the session, I'll sit with my Receiver and explore their emotions or disease, as Karol calls it, with the books.

Then we'll do a simple release as outlined by Carolyn Mein in *Releasing Emotional Patterns with Essential Oils*. I feel this primes the emotional release pump and gets the Receiver ready for their Emotional Release Raindrop.

This leaves one hour to do a Raindrop session in which we will add in the essential oil blend or single recommended by the books, along with one of two additional oils that support your goal.

Just as in the "System Supporting Raindrop," we'll start with Valor®, then go on to the cleaners (oregano and thyme), but we will omit the next three oils used in The Basic Recipe (basil, wintergreen and marjoram). This is where we will add the oil you found in *Releasing Emotional Patterns* or *The Pathway*. You can also choose to add more oils that would support or complement their release. I often use Release® and Forgiveness® as both of these oils/frequencies are so helpful for an emotional release.

As you coach your client to determine which emotion they would like to address, you may pick up on a word or oil that you feel should be added.

Now to complete the Raindrop session, you'll use cypress, peppermint, and Valor®.

CHAPTER SIX
Adding More Massage to Your Raindrop

~ For Massage Therapists ~

As a Massage Therapist, I have a hard time refraining from doing a massage for my Raindrop Receivers. I just have to work on those muscles, so I do. I always add in five to ten minutes of massage in areas that have extra tightness after all the exciting techniques that come with the application of cypress essential oil. To complete the massage time, I'll close up with palm slides and then continue with the next steps of the Raindrop, the application of Valor® and peppermint.

I've had clients ask if they could extend the massage time, so I offer a sixty minute Raindrop Massage following the steps I described above. I also offer a ninety minute Raindrop Massage in which the time for the targeted massage is now thirty to forty minutes instead of ten.

Most of the time, people are dealing with a tight neck or sore back so adding in the massage time after Thumb VitaFlex, Finger Straddle, and Stretch & Rock fits right in. Other times when the massage is needed on the front of the body, you need to do some extra planning. I'll share what I've cooked up for a ninety minute session.

I always start the session by balancing the shoulders with Valor® and setting an intention or prayer. Then I'll balance and use VitaFlex on the feet to support relaxation and get the body ready for changes. From there, I'll work on the area that needs attention. Usually it is feet, legs, iliopsoas, or SCM and scalene that clients need work on.

From there, they flip over to the prone position. I can continue the Raindrop with oregano, thyme, basil, marjoram, wintergreen and cypress. Just like I described above, after the application of cypress, followed by Thumb VitaFlex, Finger Straddle, and Stretch & Rock, I will then work on any areas on the back that need attention.

I'll end the massage part of the session with palm slides and continue with the rest of the Raindrop.

This pattern has been well received by clients. Often they will tell me they couldn't tell when the Raindrop ended and the massage began, it just flowed so smoothly.

Give a Small Raindrop Experience

There are many ways you can introduce your clients to Raindrop during their typical bodywork sessions. Just keep in mind that bodywork can be detoxing, so take the combination of Raindrop with another technique slowly for your Receiver.

For example, for a sixty minute session with someone new to Raindrop, you may do a ten minute Foot VitaFlex with a few oils to support your client's goals, and then fifty minutes of your typical body work. See how their body responds during that session after the Foot VitaFlex. Do their muscles release faster? The next day, check in with your client and see if they noticed a difference.

You could also use a few oils feathered along the spine of your client as you are doing your typical session with them. You can even add in finger circles and a few of the other techniques typically used in Raindrop. This is a great way to have your clients get a small Raindrop experience and be exposed to the oils.

I have clients that loved their small Raindrop experiences and asked for more, more, and more until they were getting a full Raindrop. Now they alternate their sessions; one visit is manual lymph drainage, the next is Raindrop.

CHAPTER SEVEN
All About the Base

Did you realize that you can tailor your Raindrop just by changing your base oil? You can!

I see the base oil choice like icing on cupcakes. You can make the same vanilla cupcake, but if you change the icing flavor you now have a different cupcake. Whether you use vanilla, chocolate, strawberry, or lemon, each icing flavor will make that vanilla cupcake a little different. You are simply tailoring your icing flavor to the tastebuds of your birthday boy or girl!

The same is true for our Raindrops.

We normally use OrthoEase™ Massage Oil Blend as a base oil because it supports the muscles of the back.

It is very common for people to replace OrthoEase™ with a base oil that does not contain any essential oils. We normally do that with the intention of reducing the amount of essential oils the Receiver is being exposed to, and to slow down absorption of the essential oils. This is often done with the goal of reducing detoxing.

In my practice, I work with a lot of physically toxic clients, so I will often use Safflower oil because I like how it feels for massage and there is little chance for allergies. Other Raindroppers commonly use coconut, almond, or Young Living's V-6™ Blend.

But have you considered using some of the other massage blends that Young Living has?

We discussed this topic in the Adapting Raindrop FaceBook Group. Here is what some of the members are doing. Look at how changing your base oil blend can tailor your Raindrop for your Receiver.

Marie Koepke shared that she uses Cel-lite Magic™ because it is a massage blend with oils that support lymph movement. If you are detoxing as you do with Raindrop you certainly want that lymph system supported!

Lorrie Papach said she uses OrthoSport™ for her son who is a wrestler. He benefits from using OrthoSport™, which is blended to support active, sore muscles.

Maximilian Gasseholm was a newlywed when this topic came up, so it was no surprise he thought of using Sensation™ massage oil! What a great idea for Valentine's or date night!

Tabatha Hubbard commented that she gave a modified Raindrop to her four-year-old and used Seedlings™ Baby Oil, which made a great base oil.

Relaxation™ Massage Oil is a great option for those who are looking for relaxation and a total "chill" experience during their Raindrop session.

Dragon Time™ massage oil is perfect for women who are working on balancing their hormones.

I hope this gives you an idea on how to tailor your Raindrops by simply switching your base oil massage blend choice!

CHAPTER EIGHT
Some more about detoxing

It has been more than fifteen years since I received my first Raindrop. My friend Alice gave it to me. I was going to massage school at the time and I'm sure she was hoping I'd add the technique into my practice. Who could have guessed what one Raindrop would lead to!

At that time, I was starting my wellness journey and I was definitely holding on to a lot of toxins. I understood detox, so when I started to get a nasty headache after my first Raindrop, I made sure I drank water. As the day went on that headache did not get better, so I just kept on drinking more and more. I remember that by 6:00 pm, I was done. My head hurt, I felt horrible, and the only thing that sounded good was going to bed, so I did. I fell asleep immediately, but I kept waking up to use the bathroom since I had drank so much water. I distinctly remember standing in the bathroom in the dark at two in the morning. The headache was much better, but I could feel these energy bands around my shoulders and elbows. They were so strong that I turned on the light to see if anything was there. I couldn't see anything around my joints, but I could feel this powerful energy.

I'm proud to say I didn't freak out or worry, I just figured it was some sort of detoxing and went back to bed. The next morning I woke up feeling great!

After receiving many Raindrops since that time, I've never felt those energy bands around my joints again. Whatever needed to be cleared had been taken care of.

We need to remember that detox, whether it is physical or emotional, will be a unique experience for each Receiver each time they receive a Raindrop. You'll never be able to duplicate a release, ever.

A Giver's Detox

We discussed how fantastic of a job our essential oils do with detoxing. They detox the Receiver, yet as the Giver, you also receive those benefits. This is important to remember when you are new to Raindrop and scheduling your sessions.

A story I tell in all my Raindrop classes offers a great example of how we, the Givers can experience detox from giving Raindrop.

After attending my first CARE Raindrop class, I started offering Raindrop in my wellness practice. I was doing one Raindrop a day, maybe three in a week, for a while and was feeling great after each session. On the day that I scheduled two Raindrops in the same day, I remember feeling fine that day and evening. However, the following morning I was late to work because my body was releasing big time and I couldn't get off the toilet! There was no pain involved at all, it was simply a grand exit of waste and toxins.

Since that time, as I've changed my diet and made improvements to my health, I have not repeated that big cleaning experience from Raindrop. It was when I volunteered to give Raindrops during the Young Living Convention one year that I realized I had come a long way in improving my health. For two days at the Convention I gave six Raindrops a day. That is a total of twelve Raindrop sessions in forty-eight hours! And you know what, I felt great and did not have any detox reactions at all.

I share this story with you to remind you that you will be receiving all the benefits the oils have to offer, so remember to take it slow in the beginning, too.

Talk It Out

In my practice, I have changed my approach to the detox discussion with my Receivers. If they experience a physical or emotional detox, the first thing we do is celebrate it! I remind them that a detox means that their body released a toxin and if they don't add it back in later, that means they are one step closer to being healthier! Celebrating a rash, quality time on the potty, or crying for a half an hour makes something that could be considered inconvenient or disheartening into an experience with a positive outcome.

Again, this is where education about the possibility of detox is so important. You want to let your Receiver have an idea about what they could experience. A headache, stuffy sinuses, an upset stomach, more bowel movements, itchiness, a skin rash, moodiness, and an emotional release are all possible.

You also want to make sure you understand your Receiver's openness to detox and be aware of their possibility of detoxing, too. That is why we have the Eight Questions to discuss with them.

PART TWO
Receiver Comfort

A Sitting Raindrop 69

Giving Raindrop Side-Lying. 77

Spinal VitaFlex on the Feet when Sitting 81

Stuffy Sinuses 83

Muscle Cramps - What to Do and How to Avoid Them 87

Prone to Sitting. 93

CHAPTER NINE
A Sitting Raindrop

Sometimes you'll work with Receivers who cannot lie on a massage table. Perhaps they are elderly and they are not able to just hop on the table. Maybe they had an injury or operation and getting on the table or lying on their stomach is too painful.

I had a client who had broken a rib. Lying prone on the table hurt them too much, and moving was painful, so we used "Raindrop at the Kitchen Table." It worked perfectly for her!

Another client of mine was going through treatment for a tumor in his esophagus. He was unable to lie prone for months because he had to have a feeding tube in order to eat while he worked on shrinking that tumor. For him, we did the side-lying Raindrop.

Knowing how to adapt to the situation and still give your Receiver a comfortable and relaxing Raindrop is important for you and your Receivers. I want you to be confident and have ideas on how to handle situations like these, because they will pop up now and then.

I do my best to use pictures and descriptions to help explain these modifications. Videos can offer additional instruction and clear up any questions you may have. For the adaptations with an accompanying video, you'll find a "Notes" section under the first photo of each adaptation, allowing you to jot down notes as you watch these videos. You can request the videos at https://AdaptingRaindrop.com/PractitionerVideos/. I hope that this will provide an easy guide for you to look back on when you need the information.

In *The Raindrop Resource Guide of Oily Families* I show families, in detail, how to do "Raindrop at the Kitchen Table." This is a simple and affordable way for families to give a comfortable and cozy Raindrop to their own family and friends even if they don't have a massage table. Don't worry, I'm not suggesting you have your Raindrop Receiver lie on the kitchen table, but instead it is an easy way to give a Raindrop to someone as they are sitting in a chair or stool and use the kitchen table as a place to rest their head and hands. I'd like to show you how to do this adaptation for two reasons.

The first is so you can pass on these tips with your Receivers. If you have a client who is very ill, they may not be able to make it to your office as often as you both feel they should. I've had many clients who I taught the basic Raindrop Technique to their spouse. They didn't have a massage table and giving a Raindrop to someone on a bed is typically a recipe for a backache for the Giver, so I showed them how to do a quick "Raindrop at the kitchen Table." Families were so appreciative.

The second reason I want to introduce this adaptation to you is because I'd like to show you how to make "Raindrop at the Kitchen Table" into a more professional, yet still comfortable and relaxing experience. When you have Receivers who cannot lie down on their stomach or back, you'll be prepared and ready for an effective alternative method.

I'll also share some handy tools you may consider adding to your Raindrop Toolbox as they will allow you to give Raindrops in many settings and still remain professional.

Raindrop at the Kitchen Table

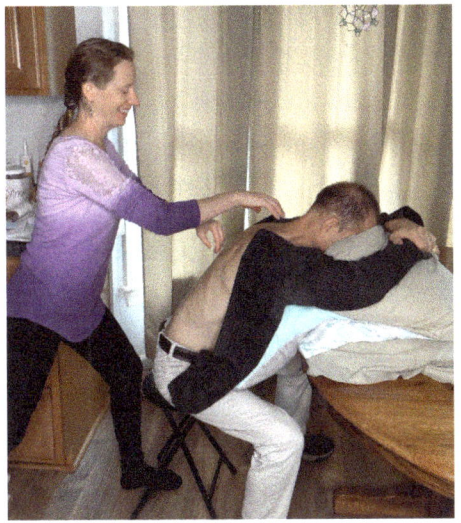
Picture # 1

By stacking up pillows on the kitchen table, you can give a nice soft place for your Receiver to lean their head, upper body, and arms against. Your Receiver will need to hug on to the pillows so they don't slide, but this gives a comfortable place for them to rest their arms. This adaptation allows you full access to their back. Your Receiver can wear a button-down shirt backwards so that their chest and arms are covered, offering modesty and warmth. See Picture #1.

This adaptation works best when your Receiver is sitting on a stool instead of a chair with a back, so the chair's back does not get in the way. Just make sure you don't have your Receiver using your wheeling massage stool, that would make for an exciting session!

When giving a Raindrop to a Receiver who is sitting, you don't need to feel restricted to using a kitchen table! You can also use your massage table or a desk. You simply need enough room to work comfortably around your Receiver. The "table" portion of this adaptation is up to you and what you have available.

All of the techniques used in Raindrop can be done when your Receiver is sitting. The adaptation you'll have to make is your stance. It is imperative that you stand with a wider base to lower your body. If you are finding yourself bending over at the waist or upper back when giving Raindrop to a Receiver who is lying on a massage table, then please take a look at *Pain-Free Raindrop* which will teach you how to correctly move and stand at a massage table so your back does not hurt.

Now let's walk through how to do all the techniques used in Raindrop for a Receiver who is sitting.

Feathering:

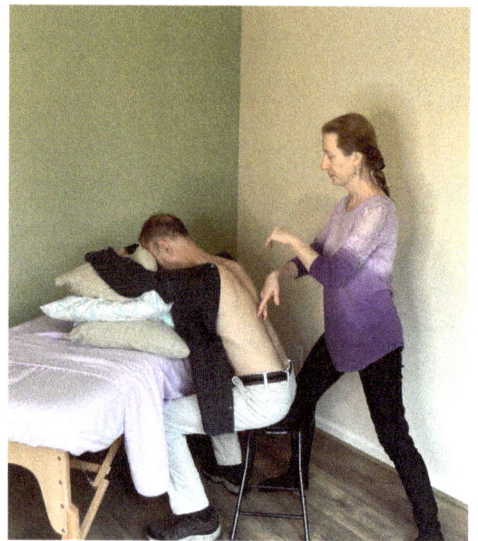

Picture # 2

The challenge with giving Raindrop to someone who is sitting versus lying prone is that the oils roll down very quickly. So the trick to making sure the drops don't roll down too far to the "no fly zone" is to drop the oils only on the upper back. You'll see how fast those drops make their way down. As you do the feathering, still from sacrum to skull, you'll stop the drops from rolling and will spread them along the spine. The trick is to get to your first feathering stroke as quickly as you can to stop the oils from rolling too far south.

The best posture to take when doing feathering is a wide stance, which will lower your body and stop you from bending at the waist (Picture # 2).

Abdominal and Cervical Support:

For the next few techniques, it is important to keep in mind that sitting in these positions does not give your Receiver abdominal support and their neck is not in alignment with their spine.

Techniques done on the abdominal area may need to be done lighter than what you are used to because your Receiver's belly and upper chest are not supported. I have found that using a pillow that is placed parallel to the Receiver's body, half on the table with the other half hanging off, gives some support.

You'll notice that your Receiver's cervical spine is bent. This means that since their neck is not in alignment with the rest of their spine, stretching the neck is avoided.

Finger Circles and Thumb VitaFlex:

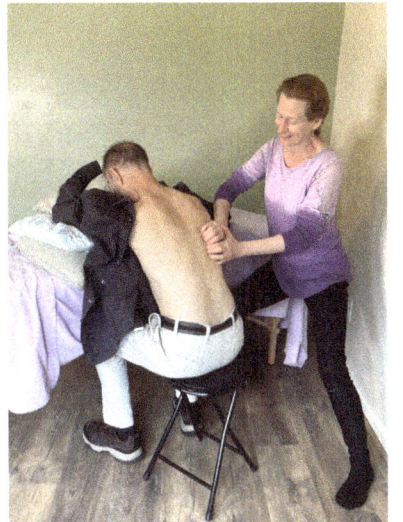

Picture # 3

You can do Finger Circles and Thumb VitaFlex the same as when your Receiver is lying face down on a massage table. The only change you'll need to make is to your posture. To do this technique on their lower back, you'll need to lower your body, and you can do this by simply taking a wider stance (Picture #3).

Stretch and Rock:

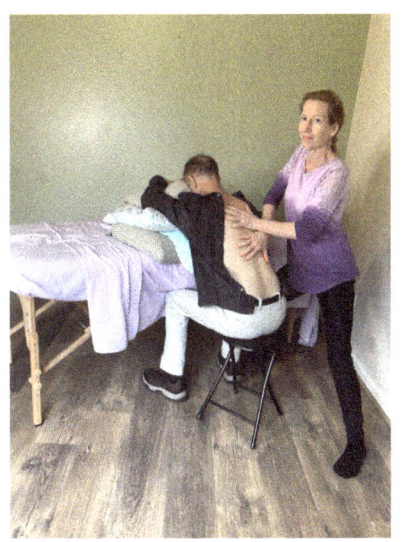

Picture # 4

You will not be able to get as much of a stretch as when a Receiver is lying on a massage table, but you can still do some. Again, the key to doing this technique when your Receiver is at the kitchen table is taking a low and wide stance. It will allow you to have more strength in your stretch than if you are bending at the waist (Picture # 4).

Avoid stretching the cervical spine in this position since the neck is bent and not in alignment with the spine.

Saw Maneuver:

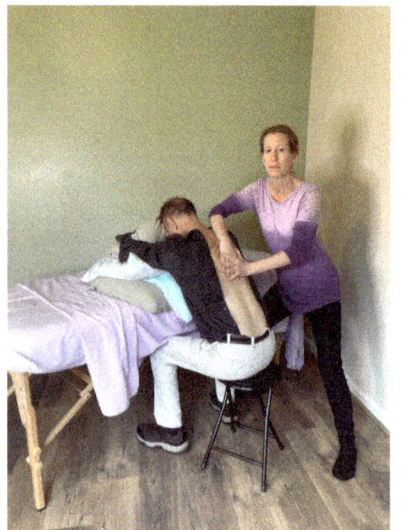

Picture # 5

The Saw Maneuver can be done from the lower back to the top of the cervical spine. You will notice that your client's body does not rock much. Stand with a wide stance to protect your back (Picture #5).

Palm Slide:

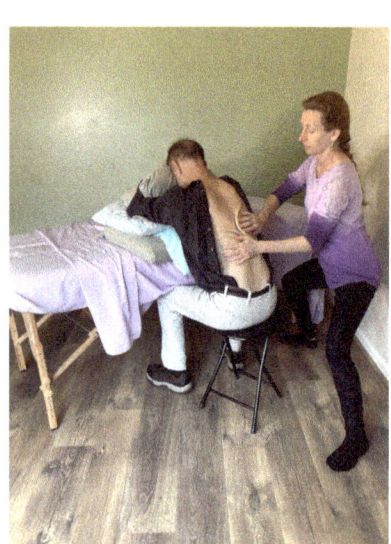

Picture # 6

This will be done the same way as if you were doing this technique to a Receiver on a massage table. Once again, the key to your strength and saving your back is a wide stance (Picture #6).

Moist Heat Pack:

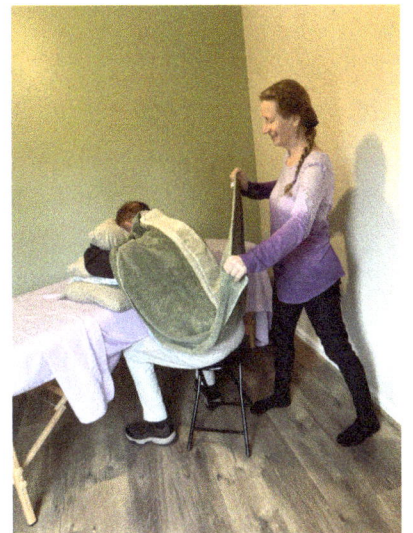

Picture # 7

You will make quite a few changes when applying the moist heat pack. To help the towels stay put and not slide down, place some of the dry towels over your Receiver's shoulders. If you use one dry towel and fold it over to make a 'hot pack sandwich,' make the fold by the sacrum. This will stop the moist towel from slipping out (Picture #7).

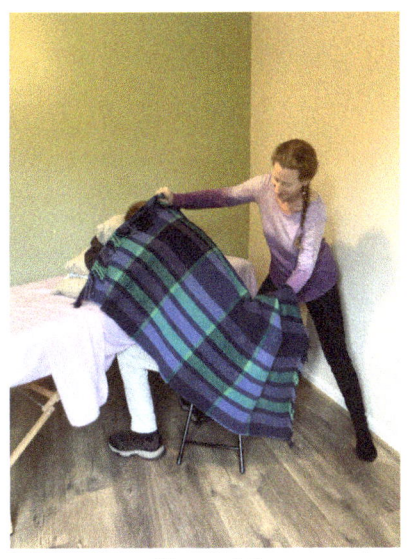

Picture # 8

To keep your Receiver warm and comfortable while they 'cook,' you of course will cover them with a sheet, blanket, or both.

Taking off the towel will be different from what you learned for a Receiver on a massage table. Here we are going to use gravity to help us! First, hold the sheet and/or blanket by your Receiver's shoulder to keep it in place. Slide your other hand under the blanket from the side and grab hold of the moist-heat-pack sandwich lying on their low back or sacrum. To remove the moist heat pack, simply pull down. It will fall quickly, so you just need to guide it out of the blanket tent (Picture #8).

Your Receiver is still covered and warm; they are toasty and comfortable. At this time, they can relax for as long as they'd like. A benefit to this technique is that your Receiver can easily stand up from the stool, and they do not need to hop off a massage table. Once they are ready, they can easily wrap themselves up in the sheet or blanket and change. If they used a button down shirt put on backwards, you can now do a button or two on the shirt so it stays on while your Receiver stands up when they are ready.

Additional Tools

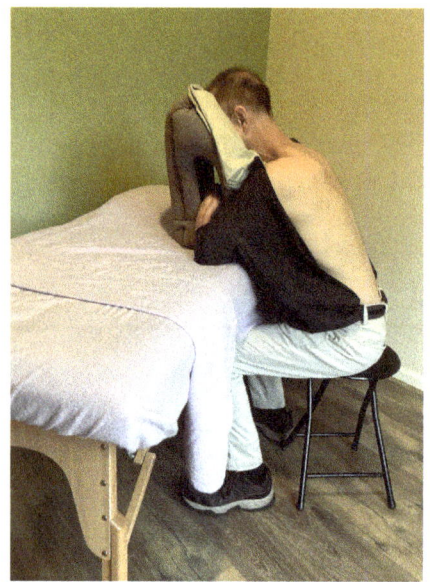

Picture # 9

I have three tool suggestions that can help you make this adaptation more professional. We'll start with the least expensive one.

The blow up travel pillow is perfect for this adaptation. It is small and compact, and inflates very quickly. I found that it works well for both adults and kids. The only drawback to this tool is that the material is not conducive to cleaning. I suggest you use a cover that can be cleaned or thrown away between clients (Picture #9).

Picture # 10 - Desktop portal with client in it.

The other tool that makes Raindrop at a table more professional is the Oakworks® Desktop Portal. The top half of this contraption is a massage chair which attaches to a table or desk. Your Receiver then sits on a stool, instead of the lower part of a massage chair. This gives your Receiver a massage face cradle to rest their head in and a firm pillow for their chest. It is quick and easy to set up and adjusts just like a massage chair so you can fit a wide variety of clients.

It is light, simple to carry with you, and is easy to store. The material is meant for repeat cleaning (Picture #10). Your Receiver simply needs to be able to sit down and stand up from a stool, with or without assistance from you. The firm chest cushion may be too firm for someone with a delicate chest or who has a big belly from pregnancy. This chest cushion does address the lack of support in the abdominal area, which now allows you to use more pressure.

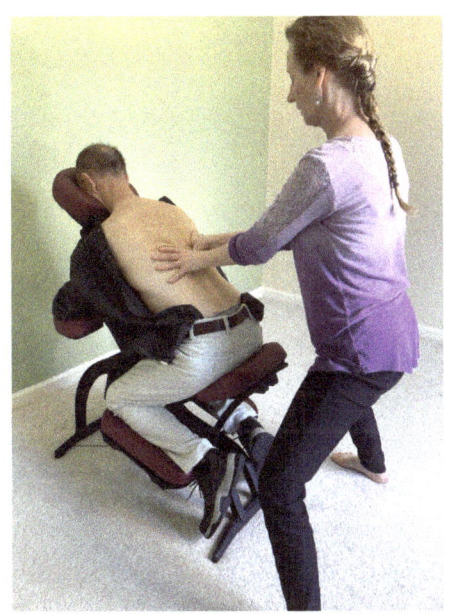

Picture # 11

The last tool I'd like to share with you is a traditional massage chair. With a massage chair, you don't need a table or desk, in fact, you don't even need a stool. All of that is taken care of by the massage chair (Picture #11).

A massage chair allows you to do a Raindrop anywhere you can find enough space for the chair and allows for you to stand and move around a bit. It makes it possible to find a private and quiet spot. Once you get the hang of it, it is also very quick and easy to set up and adjust to your Receiver. The material is meant for cleaning.

The down side to a massage chair is that it can be heavy and rather cumbersome. Traveling up and down stairs requires strength and effort. The chest pad is long and firm, not intended for pregnant women. I have also found that it requires some fancy footwork for the Receiver to straddle the seat when they are getting up and down. This is not the best choice for someone who is weak, needs assistance sitting or standing, or has poor balance.

If you end up using one of these tools in your Raindrop practice, I'd love to know. Please send me an email and let me know which one you chose and how it is working out for you.

CHAPTER TEN
Giving Raindrop Side-Lying

Side-Lying

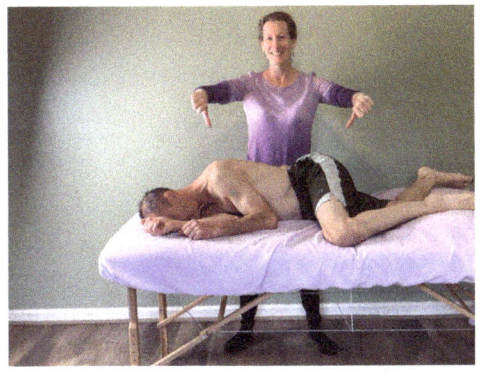
Picture # 12

It is important for you to know how to give a Raindrop to someone when they are lying on their side. I've used this technique quite a few times in my practice. Not only have I used this positioning for pregnant moms, but also for Receivers who had stomach surgery or breast surgery which did not allow them to lie face down.

You can see in Picture #12 that when someone is lying on their side, this is not a comfortable position to be lying in at all! So instead, we'll use some pillows to get them comfortable. You'll need three to four pillows.

When a Receiver is lying on their side, you'll place the first pillow under their head. This will keep their neck aligned with their spine. The goal is to get your Receiver's full spine, back, and neck parallel with the massage table. The second pillow will go between their knees to keep their legs parallel. Keeping that top leg parallel with the bottom leg, instead of leaning downward, will help to avoid lower back pain.

The last pillow will go by your Receiver's chest, which they can hold on to. Hugging onto the pillow does two things. One, it helps keep your Receiver's shoulder in good posture so it is not falling forward. Two, it offers additional modesty and warmth by covering their chest.

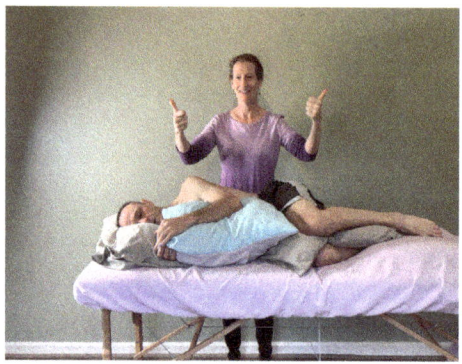

Picture # 13

You can see in Picture #13 how those pillows allow your Receiver to lie on their side comfortably. Not only will they be comfortable, in good alignment, and (if this is a pregnant mom) in a position protecting mama and baby, but you also have access to their back!

When working with a pregnant mother, depending on how big mama's belly is, you may also consider placing a small pillow, wedge, or rolled-up blanket or towel under mama's belly. This will stop her heavy belly from hanging sideways, as that can get uncomfortable, too.

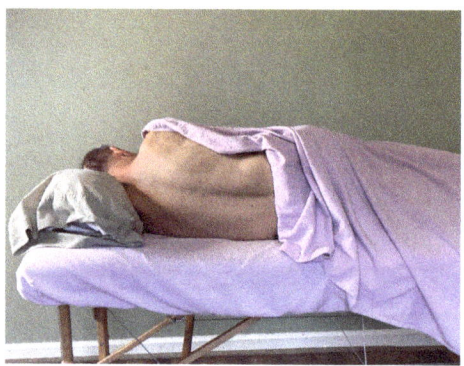

Picture # 14

Once someone is bolstered and lying in this position, only the back will be exposed, where you'll be dropping the oils and feathering them. In Picture #14, you can see Brian's back is exposed, and I can get to it easily. I put the extra sheet on his shoulder and tucked the sheet into his pants so it would not move.

How to do the Raindrop Techniques in the Side-lying Position

You can do all the techniques in the side-lying position that are normally done in Raindrop. You just need to modify or adapt the technique and your body posture to get it all done while keeping your back pain free.

Feathering:

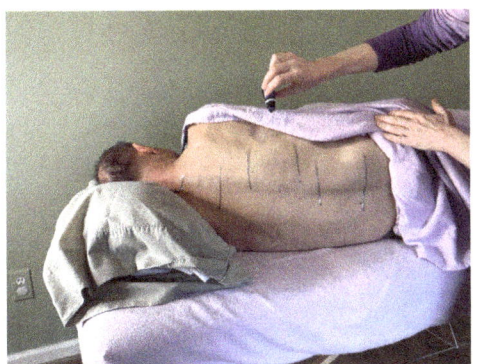

Picture # 15

As I mentioned earlier, when you drop oils along a back that is side-lying, it will be very different compared to dropping oils on a back that is lying prone. In side-lying, gravity is working against us. You'll notice that when you drop an oil, it quickly rolls down towards the massage table. You'll need to be flexible in this situation and drop above the spine, knowing that the oil will cross the spine and head towards the table (Picture #15).

It is best to work quickly. Drop those oils and start feathering right away!

Finger Circles:

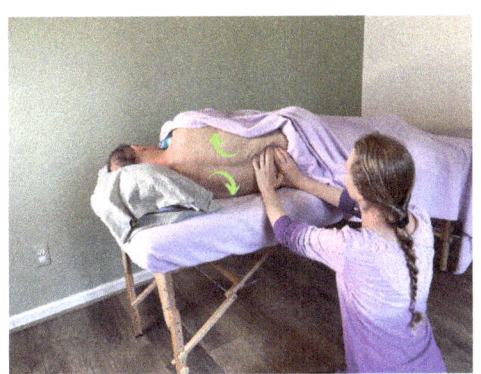

Picture # 16

When doing finger circles, you will need to be on your knees to get to the correct angle. You'll simply shuffle on your knees to move from sacrum to skull.

As always when doing this technique, you are not going to push muscles against or towards the spine. You will only push muscle away from the spine (Picture #16).

You will need to approach this technique as if you are standing on one side of the massage table and not moving from the right to the left side, as commonly taught in Raindrop classes. In this case, on the side of the spine closest to the massage table, your finger circles will have a "pull" as you rotate your fingers towards the table.

To do finger circles on the other side of the spine, the side that is farthest away from the massage table, you will circle toward the ceiling, "pulling" upwards.

Thumb VitaFlex:

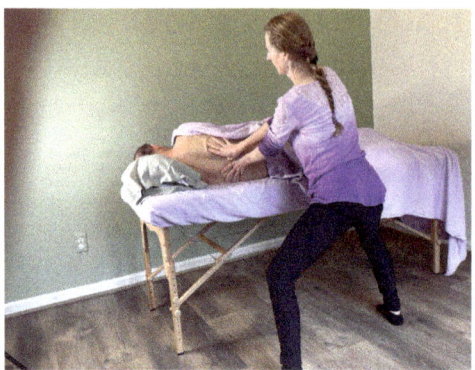

Picture # 17

This technique will be done the same way with your thumbs. The only difference will be your posture. The adaptation for this technique includes a wide base which will allow you to work lower. You create this base by having a wide stance, as shown in Picture #17. You will simply take side steps in this wide stance to move from sacrum to skull.

Saw Maneuver:

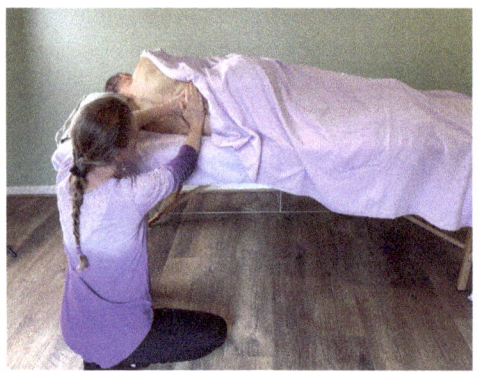

Picture # 18

Saw Maneuver will be done the same way with your stance being the only difference. It is best to do this technique on your knees (Picture #18). You'll notice that there will not be as much rocking back and forth compared to when this technique is done with the client face down. Do your best to follow the natural rhythm of your Receiver instead of forcing your rocking rhythm on them.

Stretch and Rock:

Picture # 19

Again, this technique will be done the same way, but you must change your posture. This technique will also be done on your knees. You will notice, like in Saw Maneuver, your Receiver will not shake or rock as much (Picture #19).

Palm Slide:

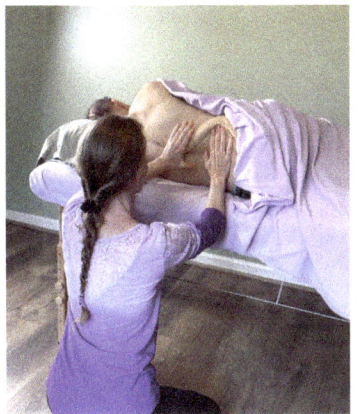

Picture # 20

This is a technique that will be abbreviated because we can't reach the full-back. You can still get tissue movement and should try to do so. The lower you are to do this technique, the stronger you will be; the kneeling position is best (Picture #20). If you are unable to get on your knees, then a rolling stool may do.

Moist Heat Pack:

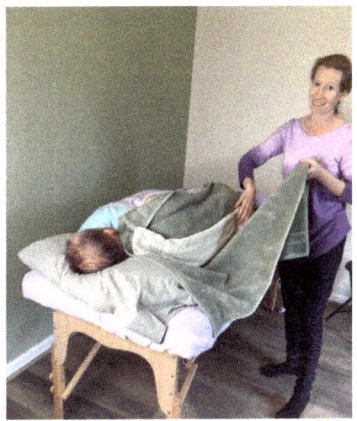

Picture # 21

Applying the moist heat pack will be similar to when your Receiver is lying on their stomach. The only difference is you are putting the towels on a sideways surface, and they may slide down a bit. To stop the towels from sliding, you can put a corner of the first layer of dry towel over your Receiver's shoulder and hip (Picture #21).

The rest of the moist-heat-pack sandwich is the same. Roll out the hot moist towel along the spine. The weight of the second dry towel stops the moist towel from sliding. Then cover with the sheet, and if you want you can add an additional blanket for extra warmth.

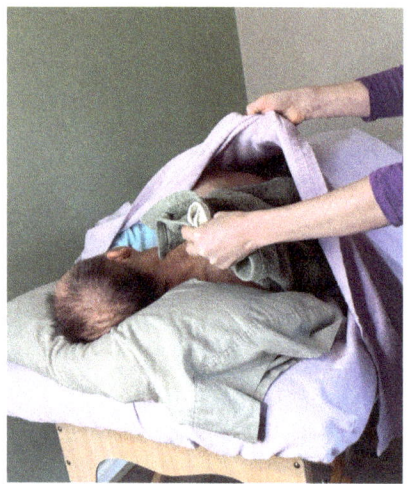
Picture # 22

Removing the moist heat pack will be done the same way as if your Receiver was lying on their stomach. Simply hold the blanket and sheet while the other hand pulls out the moist heat pack. This allows the Receiver to stay covered with sheet and blanket during and after removing the moist-heat-pack sandwich (Picture #22).

As we were taking these pictures, my husband, who was my demo, was so comfortable in this side-lying position that he fell asleep! There is no reason that you should worry that your side-lying Receiver will be uncomfortable.

CHAPTER ELEVEN
Spinal VitaFlex on the Feet when Sitting

If you do "Raindrop at the Kitchen Table" or side-lying, then you may be wondering how to do the Spinal VitaFlex on the feet, which is the first half of Raindrop.

Now don't riot, but you always have the option of skipping the Spinal VitaFlex on the feet if you need to. It all depends on your Receiver's stamina, patience, and if you feel like you need to reduce the amount of oils they are exposed to during this session.

If your Receiver can't lie on their back or hop on the massage table, you can still do Spinal VitaFlex on their feet. Let's talk about some ways you can complete this in a comfortable and effective manner.

You can use this adaptation anytime you want to do some VitaFlex on someone's feet who cannot lie on their back, a Receiver who is unable to get on a massage table, or for a Receiver who needs to lie on their side.

If your Receiver is sitting on a chair, you can simply sit on the floor and access their feet.

Your Posture

Depending on what your Receiver is sitting on, say a chair, couch, or massage table, that will affect their foot height. The height of your Receiver's foot will affect your posture. It is important to have correct posture while doing Foot VitaFlex. Your posture will either make this time a pleasant or an uncomfortable experience. It will also affect your VitaFlex technique; if you have good posture and no pain, you'll do a much better job.

The Practitioner's Raindrop Resource Guide

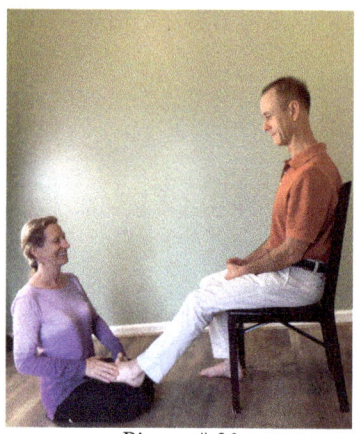

Picture # 23

To determine if you have good posture or need to make adjustments to your positioning, look at your shoulders while you are doing Foot VitaFlex. If one of your shoulders is not raised or lowered, and you are able to sit up straight, that is the perfect height for the Receiver's foot (Picture #23).

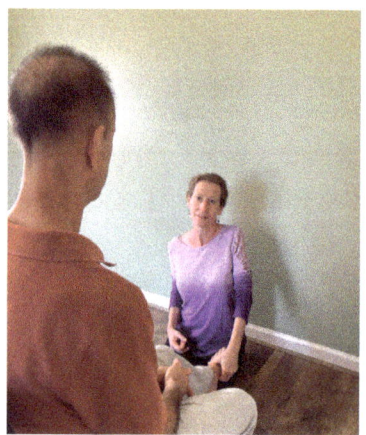

Picture # 24

If you find that while doing Foot VitaFlex, the shoulder of your VitaFlexing arm is rising to your ear that means your Receiver's foot is too high for you (Picture #24).

You'll find that when you lower the Receiver's foot, your shoulder should drop. Your neck will thank you for this improved posture.

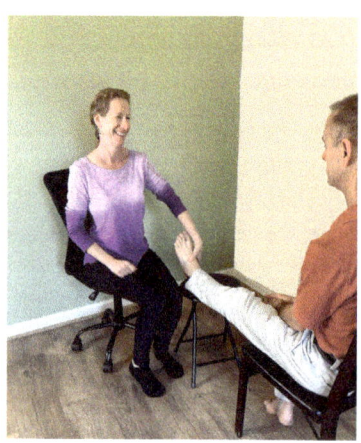

Picture # 25

If your Receiver is sitting in a chair, I would recommend sitting on the floor, like in Picture #23. If you are not comfortable getting down on the floor, then no worries, you can still offer Foot VitaFlex to your Receiver without issue. You can see in Picture #25 I used a chair along with a stool. I like the adjustable rolling chair because it gives me the ability to move around easily, and also gives me the chance to raise or lower my body to put the Receiver's foot in a comfortable location for me to work with.

This makes it easy to then offer Foot VitaFlex to your Receiver if they are sitting in a chair or on a massage table. You'll just need a stool for the Receiver's foot to be propped up on.

The goal is to have both the Giver and Receiver comfortable. Keeping your shoulders in a neutral position will help keep you comfortable, which will allow you to give a better VitaFlex and be more attentive to your Receiver's needs.

Like in a traditional Raindrop, when you switch to the other foot, you'll also need to switch your VitaFlexing hand. This is where having a rolling chair is convenient. You can just roll on over to the other foot.

CHAPTER TWELVE
Stuffy Sinuses

One of the most common complaints from Raindrop Receivers is that their sinuses get stuffy. I'm sure you have found that when most people are lying face down on a massage table, they will get congested to some degree.

What makes Raindrop unique is that one of the signs of cleansing or detoxing that may come with Raindrop is sinus drainage or sinus congestion. When you put these two together, lying prone for a long period of time plus detoxing, you have an excellent chance for your Receiver to get super congested sinuses!

When I started offering Raindrop I'd feel bad at the end of the session when I applied the moist heat pack to my clients who developed super congested sinuses. I didn't have another option for them, they just had to struggle through it. After a while I figured I had to do something different for them. This time on the table is supposed to be relaxing and enjoyable for my Receiver. They should not feel like they simply have to suffer through this moist heat pack time.

With my clients who I knew would get stuffy, I started asking them if they would prefer to flip over one more time to lie on the table supine for their moist heat pack. Oh my, were they excited to hear that they had another option and were more than willing to do an extra flip and maneuvering on the table if that meant they could lie face up again for the last ten minutes of their session!

This led me to the decision to offer this option to all my Raindrop Receivers. I simply ask them when it comes time for the moist heat pack, "The last part of Raindrop is a moist heat pack applied to your back. You'll be lying face down for another five to ten minutes. If you prefer, you can lie face up or just stay face down, it is up to you. What would you like to do?" About nine times out of ten, my Receivers are more than happy to stay face down for another ten minutes. But I'm so glad I asked when the rare tenth one says, "Oh yes, please I'd be much more comfortable lying face up! What do I need to do?" I know that their session will be more enjoyable just because I asked.

There are a couple steps to getting your Receiver to lie in the supine position and get a moist heat pack under their spine, which includes two ways to help them into this position.

Step One - Flipping them Over:

If your Receiver chooses to lie on their back for the moist heat pack, then the first thing you'll need to do is assist them in turning over.

When a Receiver flips over from their stomach to their back, it is always helpful to hold up the sheet just a few inches so they don't get tangled in the sheet while flipping.

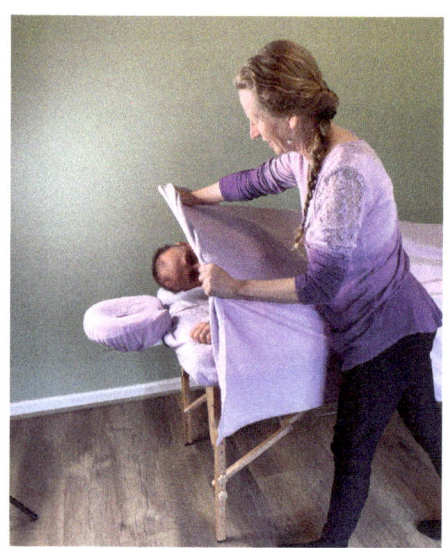

Picture # 26

Ask them to scoot down before flipping over. This allows them to have their head on the massage table instead of the cradle after flipping over. You'll notice in Picture #26 that I can only see the top of my Receiver's head after they scooted down a bit. This way they will stay toasty warm and covered, too.

Once that is done, and they are now lying face up, you'll need to get your dry towel and hot, moist towel to make the moist-heat-pack sandwich.

Step Two - Moist Heat Pack:

There are two ways you can coach your Receiver to move so you can position the moist heat pack for them to lie on.

Option #1 Sitting Up

The first option is to coach your Receiver to simply sit up. Before your Receiver starts to sit up, ask them to take their arms out from under the sheets. This will allow them to keep that sheet close to their body when they are sitting up for a few minutes.

A tip to make sitting up from a lying position easier is to ask your Receiver to bend their knees first. If you are strong enough and have a sturdy back, you can also offer your arm for assistance in pulling up.

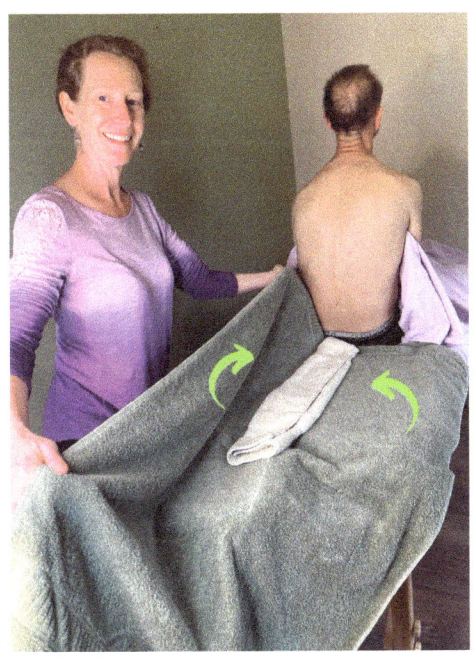

Picture # 27

Once your Receiver is sitting up you now have access to the table and their back. You can easily lay out the dry towel, then the moist hot towel and finish with the dry towel on top. When you lay out the moist-heat-pack sandwich, make sure you start it right at your Receiver's sacrum. Stand at the head of the massage table and check to ensure the spine is in alignment with the towel. Make adjustments to the towel as needed (Picture #27).

When your moist heat pack is in the correct position, you can assist your Receiver in lying back down.

The temperature you normally use for a moist heat pack when a Receiver is lying face down may be too hot for someone who is lying upon it. It may be a good idea to use two layers of dry towel between your Receiver's back and the moist hot towel. This can be accomplished by folding your dry towel into three sections, as shown in Picture #27. You could also just allow that moist hot towel to cool a bit before making the moist-heat-pack sandwich.

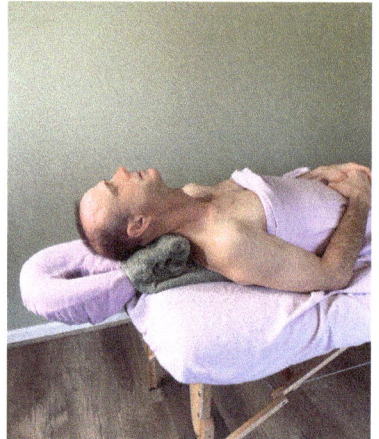

Picture # 28

I recommend rolling up the towels by the head to make a pillow which will sit in the curve of your Receiver's neck. This will allow their neck to have moist heat on it too, and it feels so good! (Picture #28)

Option #2 Roll to the Side

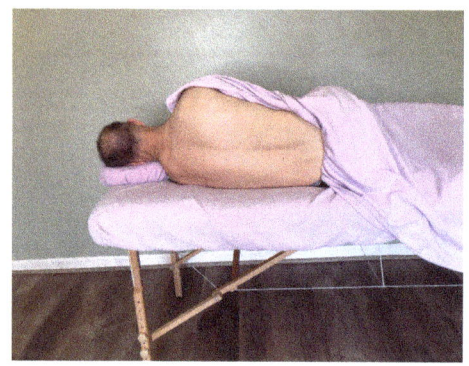

Picture # 29

The second option is to ask your Receiver to roll to their side and lie on their side for a few minutes while you lay out the moist heat pack for them. (Picture #29) This is a good option for those who struggle sitting up. In order to see their spine, you will then need to pull back the sheet to expose their back from neck to waist. The next step is to make a moist-heat-pack sandwich on the table and then have them lie back on it.

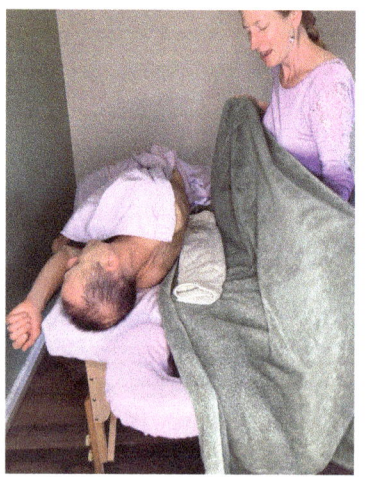

Picture # 30

To make this easy, lay the dry towel down parallel to your Receiver's back. Half of the dry towel should be on the table, while the other half is hanging off the side (Picture #30). Next, lay out the hot moist towel and then fold the remaining half of the dry towel to cover the moist towel.

Remember, you might want to consider doubling up the dry towels atop the moist towel since the moist hot pack will feel warmer to your Receiver with their body weight pressing down on it. When it is time for the Receiver to lie on the moist heat pack, I go one step further to make sure that my Receiver's spine is actually on the moist towel. I place one hand on the towel where the small of their back will rest and the other hand where their neck will be. When they lie on their back again, the moist heat pack and my hands will be under their spine. Having my hands under them momentarily will keep that heat pack from sliding around, and I'll also be able to feel with the top of my hands if the pack really is under their spine. This also gives me another indication on how hot those towels are. Due to the curvature of the low back and neck, it is easy for me to pull my hands out.

Just like in Picture #28, roll up the extra towel to create a neck pillow that will offer moist heat to the cervical region of your Receiver's spine.

From here, your job is done. Your Receiver can lie on that moist heat pack without their sinuses being stuffy and painful!

Tips from Raindroppers

If your Receiver is comfortable lying face down for an additional ten minutes, then go ahead and apply that moist heat pack without concerns. If your Receiver does seem a bit stuffy, you might consider using one of these tips from fellow Raindroppers who shared what they do when their Receiver has stuffy sinuses.

Leslie Vornholt: Place a drop of peppermint or eucalyptus on a cotton pad that they can breathe in while face down on the table.

Carolyn McCrary: When I have a client lying on their stomach with the moist heat pack, I'll VitaFlex the sinus reflexes at the neck of the toes. When they get up I'll VitaFlex the sinuses on the forehead and sinus areas across the cheeks. It usually opens them immediately.

Lisa Storm: Our instructor said to put an oil such as RC®/Raven™ Blend behind the ear. Massage their neck with eucalyptus so they can smell it.

CHAPTER THIRTEEN
Muscle Cramps - What to Do and How to Avoid Them

Another issue that may pop up now and then is your Receivers complaining of having calf cramps or their lower back hurting while they are either supine or prone on your table.

When I first started offering bodywork I remember clients clutching calves or yowling because they had a foot cramp. Goodness, I felt horrible that they were in that pain and that I couldn't fix it for them right away. It took a few years into my practice for me to connect the dots between muscle cramps and posture. When I discussed my muscle cramp "ah-ha" with my husband, he enlightened me even more! I wish he and I had that conversation years earlier.

This chapter will give you all the insights that helped me know how to deal with muscle cramps like a pro. You don't need to stand there feeling anxious and helpless like I did those first few years. It is not a matter of if, but when, a Receiver has a muscle cramp. I want you to have an idea of why it may be happening and feel confident on how to help them.

First I'd like to explain why they may be experiencing these muscle cramps and that will help you understand how best to reduce the chance that the cramps arise at all!

Why do Muscles Cramp?

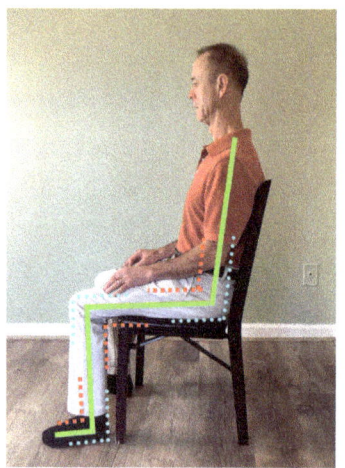

Picture # 31 - Sitting angles and muscles

Most of us spend a lot of time sitting. We sit in the car, at the table, watching TV, and, many of us, at our jobs. Over time muscles get used to this sitting position. If you look at someone who is sitting, you'll notice that there are three ninety-degree angles that are formed. One at the ankles, one at the knees, and the third at the hips (Picture #31).

The muscles on the "inside" of the angle are shortened, and the muscles that make up the "outside" of the angle are lengthened.

When you ask someone who has been in a sitting posture for the last ten years of their life for eight hours a day, to lie flat on a massage table, the muscles that have been shortened are now being asked to be lengthened out all the way. How often do those muscles lengthen like that for a long period of time? If the person is getting cramps, that lets you know not very often! Those muscles have gotten "stuck" in this shortened position and are responding with cramping or aching.

To fix this, we use bolsters or pillows.

Calf Cramps

Picture # 32

Let's take a look at calf cramps. You can see that when someone is sitting, the hamstring and calf muscles are shortened (Picture #32). When they are lying supine (face up), that joint is open and those muscles are lengthened (Picture #33).

Have you ever had someone jump off your table because their calf was cramping? Oh my goodness, that sure does

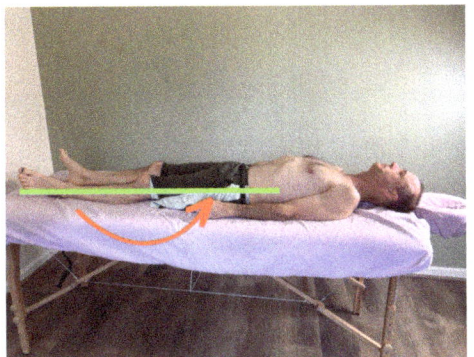

Picture # 33

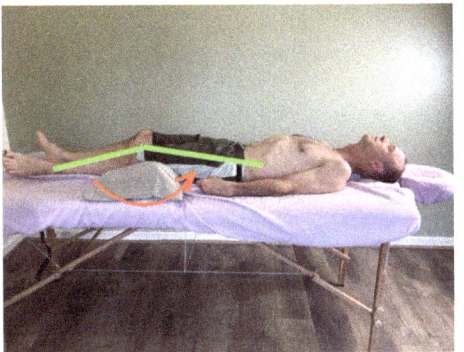

Picture # 34

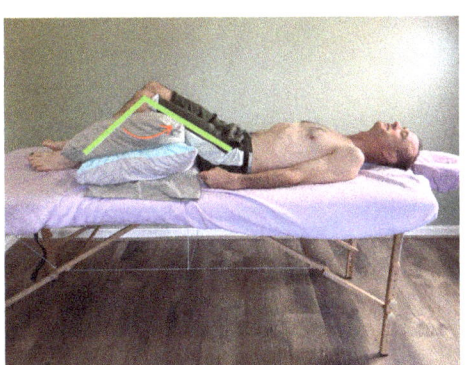

Picture # 35

create an exciting time and negates the whole relaxing experience we are looking for with Raindrop!

This is what you need to do. You need to get those muscles back into their comfortable posture, which is shortened. Place pillows under your Receiver's knees to shorten the hamstring and calf muscles (Picture #34). If your Receiver is having a calf cramp even with a pillow, that means you need to bolster them further. Put another pillow under their knees, even two more if you need to. You'll notice that as you put more bolsters under the knees, their legs are getting back into that sitting position (Picture #35).

Besides using essential oils to help relax muscles, adding more bolsters will help to reduce those calf cramps.

Foot Cramps

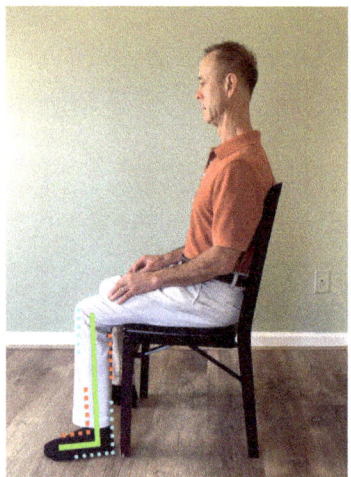

Picture # 36 - Ankle Joint

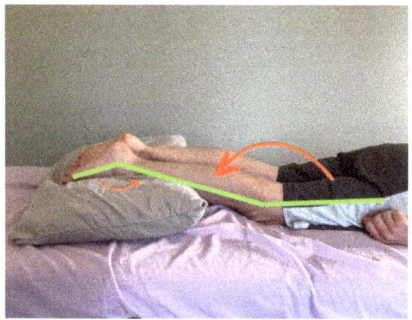

Picture # 37 - Ankle Bolstered

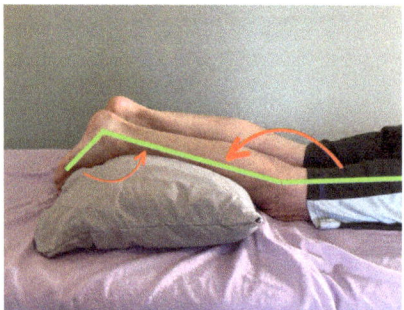

Picture # 38 - Ankle Bolstered with 90 angle

Foot cramps are common. If you look, the ankle is simply another angle (Picture #36). There are quite a few muscles from the lower leg that travel across the ankle joint and attach onto the foot. Not only do many muscles that make up the calf cross the ankle, but there are muscles in the front of the leg that also cross the ankle and attach to various places on the foot.

When someone is lying supine, instead of a cramp being in the calf, the calf muscles can tighten and create a cramp in the foot. Bending the knee with a bolster and reducing the stretch of the calf can help ease foot cramping.

Often we'll put pillows under our Receiver's ankles when they are face down. This is also creating that bend in the knee, which will put the lower leg muscles into a "sitting position" again (Picture #37).

If your Receiver is still having foot cramps while in the prone position, it could be due to the location of the pillow under their ankles. Often we put the pillow under the ankles in a location that pulls on the muscles in the front of the lower leg. The pillow is putting the ankle joint in a wider angle than it is used to. This is causing a pull on the muscles located in the front of the lower leg. To fix this, simply move the pillow up so that the ankle is once again at a ninety degree angle (Picture #38).

Lower Back Pain

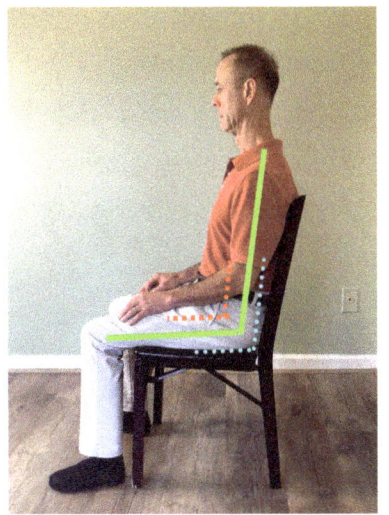

Picture # 39 - Angle of Hips

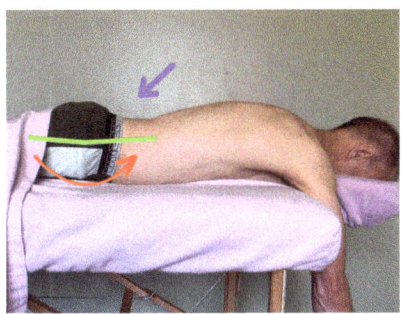

Picture # 40 - Prone - Low Back Pain

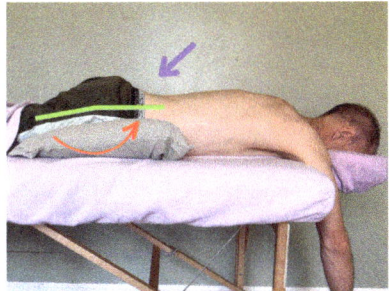

Picture # 41 - Prone with pillow under hips

The common cause of lower back pain for someone who is lying prone is again, tight muscles. In Picture #39, take a look at the angle that is created in the hips when someone is sitting. The back and glute muscles are stretched and the abdominal and quad muscles are shortened.

When someone is lying face down, those abdominal and upper leg muscles are stretched out. If the massage table is padded and soft, this may actually cause the inner angle to open wider than 180 degrees as the tummy sinks into the table (Picture #40). This postural change is often felt as lower back pain. To bring those stretched muscles into a position they are used to, place a pillow under the hips. Not the stomach, but hips (Picture #41). This is only a slight change, but for Receivers who are super tight and experiencing back pain while prone, this is enough to help the muscles get back into their state of comfort and relieve that pain.

What about low back pain when someone is lying supine? How do you use pillows to change the hip angle? Most likely the pain they are experiencing can be relieved by placing pillows under the knees. This allows the hamstrings to shorten again,

The Practitioner's Raindrop Resource Guide

which has a direct affect on the lower back muscles (Picture #35).

Neck Pain

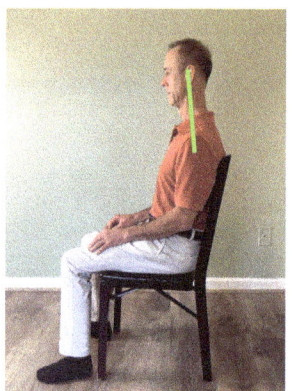

Picture # 42 - Sitting angles neck and head

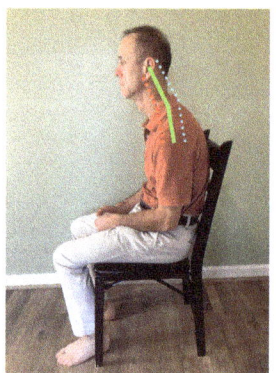

Picture # 43 - Head forward

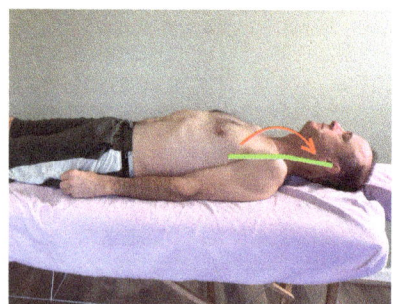

Picture # 44 - Supine neck no bolster

Another complaint you may hear from Receivers as they lie face up is that their neck hurts or is not comfortable. Often, your Receiver may point to the front of their neck as they tell you they are uncomfortable.

Where the neck meets our shoulders creates another joint. If someone has head-forward posture, the muscles in the front of the neck and chest are shortened and the muscles in the back are stretched out (Picture #42 & 43).

Look at what happens when someone lies supine. The muscles in the front are asked to stretch out (Picture #44). If they are not used to that posture, those muscles will yell and complain which translates to pain or discomfort.

By placing pillows placed under the head, you bring the head into a forward position, shortening those front neck muscles. This brings the muscles back into the posture they are more familiar with (Picture #45).

Don't get me wrong, I'm not saying that this Receiver should stay in the head forward posture forever. We want their muscles to adjust and change so that they can have all the benefits that come with better

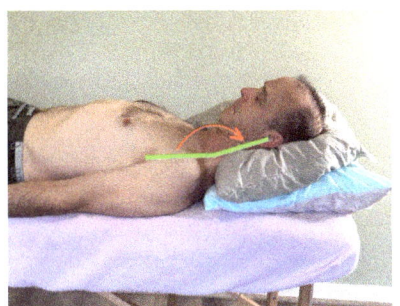
Picture # 45 - Supine head bolstered

posture. But if they are uncomfortable during this session, it will not be a pleasant experience. Our goal is to help them relax so that their muscles can relax. We need them to receive this Raindrop and additional Raindrops so that the oils, our emotional release work, and/or muscle release work can facilitate the body to adjust to its natural state, which translates to better posture!

One pillow, two pillows, three pillows, more?

You'll be surprised with some Receivers who are super tight just how much of an angle their muscles require to be comfortable. You may need to use not one, but two or three pillows to bring them to a position of comfort.

Pro Tip:

Now that you are familiar with these "sitting body angles," watch how your Receiver walks into your space and observe their posture. If you notice these angles in your Receiver's posture, you'll know that they may need some extra bolsters to stay comfortable on your table. You may find that older Receivers with poor posture have muscles that simply do not like to lay flat anymore. With continued Raindrops along with your healing gifts, they may make huge strides in their posture.

CHAPTER FOURTEEN
Prone to Sitting

Sometimes when you finish a Raindrop, you'd like to be able to stay with your Receiver as they get up from lying face down to sitting to standing. This may be because your Receiver is ill, elderly, completing their first Raindrop experience, or they mentioned they were feeling dizzy or woozy.

If your Receiver is wearing a shirt backwards, that makes it easy to keep them covered and modest when they sit up. All you need to do is close a few buttons on their shirt and proceed in helping them up.

As they are sitting on the table, you can offer them a glass of water and stay with them until they feel confident about standing up safely.

If your Receiver is not wearing a shirt, you can easily use the sheet to keep them covered as they maneuver to sitting. Let's walk through how you can coach your Receiver to move from prone to sitting to standing while keeping them covered the whole time.

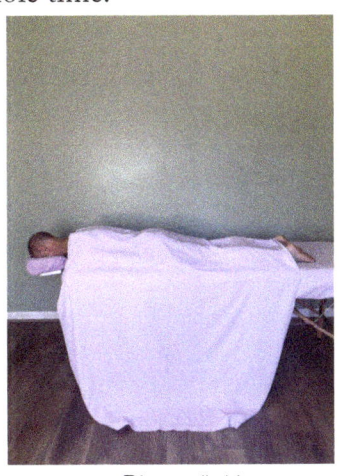

Picture # 46

First, you'll remove the bolster from under their ankles to allow easier movement. Then rotate the top sheet so that it is perpendicular to the table instead of parallel (Picture #46). Rotating the sheet this way will now expose their feet, but will allow full body coverage when they sit up.

Now, ask your Receiver to swing their legs off the massage table towards you

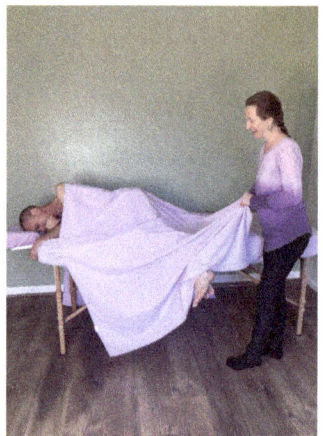

Picture # 47

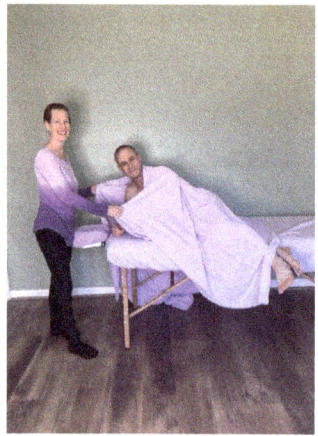

Picture # 48

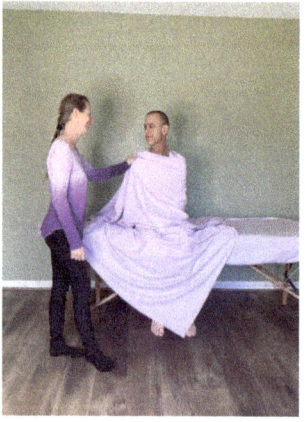

Picture # 49

(Picture #47). The next step is to ask them to sit up. As they are pushing themselves up, you will use one hand to hold the "front" side of the sheet so that it stays against their chest and use your other hand to keep the "back" side close to their body (Picture #48).

Once they are sitting up, you can hold both sides of the sheet with one of your hands near their shoulder. This will keep them covered and modest so the two of you can talk and you can determine when they are ready to stand up. This position of the sheet provides enough coverage that you can still be with them when they are standing (Picture #49). Once you both agree that the Receiver can be alone safely and get dressed, they can reach up and hold the sheet around themselves while you leave to give them privacy.

This technique can also be used for Receivers when they are lying on their side. They simply need to swing their legs off the massage table and then sit up. Sitting up from a side-lying position is easier than from face down.

PART THREE
Special Considerations

Amputation	98
Autism	98
Babies and Toddlers	99
Brain	102
Cancer	102
Children	107
Cortisone Injections for Pain	108
Edema vs Lymphedema	109
Emotional Release and Trauma Response	109
Multiple Sclerosis (MS) and Other Conditions Affecting the Myelin Sheath	113
Neuropathy	113
Nursing	113
Obesity	115
Pregnancy	116
Scoliosis	119
A Growing Resource	121

CHAPTER FIFTEEN
Special Considerations

This chapter on Special Considerations does not have a fully inclusive list, and it is not meant to. I didn't intend this chapter to be like the *Essential Oils Desk Reference* because the previous chapters give you the tools to tailor your Raindrops for many common wellness concerns.

This chapter is meant to share tips, adaptations, or stories to help you add or modify your Raindrops when giving them to someone with a 'special consideration.'

Some of these tips have come from my experiences as I worked with clients and family. Other tips were shared with me, and I thought you'd be interested in them since they taught me huge lessons! You'll also find some advice from other Raindroppers that I will pass on to you.

This is a chapter that I envision will grow as more people read this resource guide. I'd love for you to send me your tips and stories on how you adapted a Raindrop to support a unique need. You can always submit a tip or story to AdaptingRaindrop.com. As I receive your tips and stories, I'll add them in the new edition, and, with your permission, I would like to give you credit.

I put these tips in alphabetical order to make them easier to find.

Many of these 'special considerations' can be hot topics. I have seen them create discourse and disagreement because there are so many views regarding essential oil use. My tips and feelings on these special considerations are not the only views so take and use what feels good and right to you.

Amputation

I have not had the opportunity to use this tip yet, but it makes so much sense when you learn about our body's energy field. When working with someone who is experiencing phantom pain after an amputation, do VitaFlex as if the limb was there. It has been reported that VitaFlexing the aura of the missing limb eliminated phantom pain for some Receivers. When combining oils and VitaFlex, there is so much energy involved in Raindrop. It does not surprise me that these techniques would help restore the connection of a wounded aura.

Autism

The Autism Spectrum is wide, and once again, each person who has been diagnosed is unique. As with each Receiver, it is imperative that you apply the information given in Part One. Ask those questions and consider the concepts to determine how much oil and perhaps which oils to use. It may be more appropriate to ask the mother or caregiver these questions and explain the concepts behind each question.

My experience giving Raindrop to kids on the spectrum has always been pleasantly positive. During our time together, moms were always surprised at how well their child enjoyed Raindrop.

A common behavior of those diagnosed with severe autism is tactile sensitivity—sensitivity to new types of touch or textures, and not wanting to be touched, especially by a new person. Another common behavior of those on the spectrum is desiring constant movement.

Both of these common behaviors, tactile sensitivity and need for movement, seem to negate that whole idea of giving someone a Raindrop who has severe autism. I have given this technique to three young clients diagnosed with severe autism, who received it willingly with enjoyment.

What I did was skip the Foot Vita Flex and started with feathering on the back. I decided to skip working on the feet because feet tend to be an extremely sensitive area. Lying face down always helps my adult clients relax, so I thought this would help these boys, too, and it did.

Before we started, I told the boys that they were in total control of how long they stayed on the massage table. I let them know that when they wanted the Raindrop to stop, all they needed to say was "I'm all done," and they were free to get up. This worked well, and they stayed on the table longer than I expected.

The feathering technique is magic and does a wonderful job at stimulating the parasympathetic nervous system, which supports the relaxation of the body's systems. All three of these kids loved the feathering techniques and voluntarily stayed still on the table for twenty to forty-five minutes. This time of peaceful relaxation was appreciated by both their moms and the boys. As they became more comfortable with Raindrop with repeat visits, their time on the table increased.

Please consider teaching caregivers how to do the Raindrop Technique, as this is a wonderful bonding opportunity between parents and their children.

Babies and Toddlers

Babies are small, and their systems are new and more sensitive than a child or an adult. The big key to remember for babies is to dilute, decrease, and go slow.

Start with diluting at least 50/50, and only use one to two oils and see how the baby responds. Are you going to do a full Raindrop on a baby? No way, but you can use this technique to apply oils to these little bodies and see wonderful results.

Most babies would receive Raindrop to support their digestive system, respiratory system, immune system, or to help them relax.

Keep in mind that giving Raindrop to babies offers such a perfect bonding time between babies and their caregivers. As professionals, I see our roles as teachers; we teach caregivers how to give Raindrops to their babies. I will admit, the idea of snuggling up with a baby to give them a little Raindrop sounds like the best Raindrop session ever, but give parents that gift of bonding and allow them to gain confidence by using the oils to support their little one's total health. These same tips I will share with you here can be used until the baby is a toddler.

Here is how we can mentor caregivers to give Raindrops to babies so it is a relaxing and enjoyable experience.

The Adaptations:

How do you give a Raindrop to a little squirmy baby or toddler without dropping oil bottles, babies crawling away, and toddlers crying? This is how!

The first step is to GET ORGANIZED. You should have everything that you need for this Raindrop within arm's reach. Ideally, at the end of this Raindrop, mama and their little one will have time to relax, cuddle, and maybe even nap together.

Mama will need within arm's reach:
- The base oil
- A small bowl for each oil that will be used. You will dilute your oils ahead of time and have them ready to use in the bowls
- A warm blanket

The best time to give little ones a Raindrop is when they are sleepy and relaxed. I have found that bath time is a perfect prelude to Raindrop. Not only does this help little ones to relax and get warm, but they are also naked, and you have easy access to their back.

It is important to get everything ready before bath time, and then when the bath is done, Mama should go to her Raindrop location. This may be a comfortable rocking chair or the bed.

Mama will position the baby over her shoulder, like if she were going to burp them. With the Raindrop tools by her side ready to use, she can reach for the base oil and apply some on the little one's back. This application of base oil will slow the absorption of the essential oil and make sure there is no discomfort from the phenols doing their job. To apply the base oil, Mama will just put a few drops in one hand and rub it on the baby's back.

The Essential Oil Application:

Have the essential oils and base oil blended in the small bowls diluted as decided on. Each essential

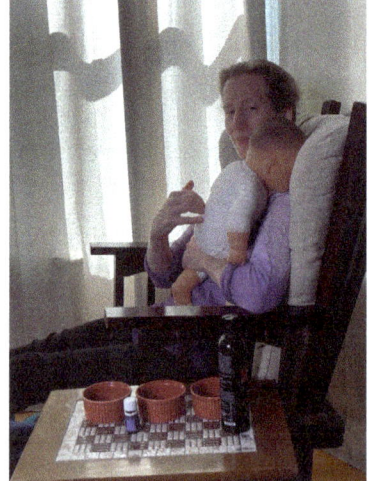

Picture # 50

oil will be mixed with a base oil in an individual bowl. You just need to dip the fingers of one hand in a bowl and then apply that blend on the baby's back by feathering it in (Picture #50).

That feathering will be calming for the baby, just like it is for you. Ideally, Mama should turn her hand and use her nails to feather, if that is not possible, she can use her finger tips. Either way, the feathering will stimulate the baby's nerves exiting the spine. The baby is getting all the benefits of Raindrop; essential oils and nerve stimulation. The slower the feathering is, the more calming and relaxing it is for the baby!

Do that with each oil chosen.

Picture # 51

If the baby is up for more, Mama can also do some gentle finger circles. In Picture #51, I am doing finger circles on the baby's left side. I can easily do finger circles on the baby's right side by moving my hand/fingers to the other side of her spine. Remember, the 'pull' will always be away from the spine.

The slower the circles are, the more relaxing it is for the baby. Each side can be done one time, two times, or three times. It all depends on time and how receptive the little one is.

Other techniques typically used in Raindrop will not be used here. Mama can always do some large circles with her palm on the baby's back. Who doesn't find that super relaxing?

I'm going to suggest Mama skips the moist heat pack. Instead, I would have her grab that warm blanket and cover up the baby and herself. Now the two can just take a nap together.

In the pictures, I was sitting in a rocking chair. This can also be done lying on a bed with the little one on Mama's tummy. Another option is to have both lying on their sides, like when nursing. In the cold winter, I sat on the toilet in the bathroom because I didn't want to leave the warm bathroom. Once the Raindrop was done, it was easy to move to the bed and cover up with more blankets. As with anything, when it comes to little ones, be flexible and do what works for Mama and baby!

Toddlers:

This method can still be used as the baby grows into a toddler. The caregiver may not be able to hold their toddler up on their shoulder, but the little one can sit facing Mama on her lap with their legs on either side of Mama. This will give Mama access to their little one's back for the Raindrop and some wonderful cuddling time.

Brain

For those Receivers who need support for their brain function, such as with Traumatic Brain Injury (TBI), Down Syndrome, strokes, or Parkinson's Disease, I'd like to share a tip that I received from Dr. David Stewart. He suggested that when you are doing feathering, instead of stopping at the occipitals or base of the skull, keep on feathering the head up to the Receiver's crown or top of the head.

Do this extended feathering for each oil and each time you do feathering. Consider using oils that support oxygenation and oils that target that Receiver's specific needs/goals.

Cancer

This is a topic that has many opinions and views. Thank you for letting me express mine here.

If someone has been diagnosed with cancer, it is very important that you discuss the detoxing questions with them in Chapter Two and modify your Raindrop accordingly.

Anyone who has received this diagnosis is most certainly full of emotions. This path contains countless questions and decisions that develop into a unique journey. Not everyone is going to make the choices you would make.

It is paramount that as a Raindropper, you need to educate your Receiver and allow them to be involved in the decisions and goals regarding Raindrop. It is the best situation for all involved to work with the support of a Natural Wellness Professional who is open to essential oils and Raindrop. That way you have someone to discuss oil choices with and help if there is a detox reaction. Raindrop itself is not a cure-all, but it can greatly support wellness goals.

I've worked with clients who, once they received the cancer diagnosis, started a dramatic cleansing and detox protocol with medical support. They were doing daily colon cleanses, eating clean, and their body was prepared to manage additional toxins the phenols kicked up during their Raindrop. They were ready for additional cleansing and came to me with that intention.

I've also worked with clients diagnosed with cancer who were very sickly, and their body was not ready to process any toxic load. With this client, I saw my primary role was to support their lymphatic system so it could allow the body to remove the toxic overload their body was holding onto.

In the Adapting Raindrop Facebook Group, Sherian McCoy shared a helpful tip of which I was unaware. She said, "I am a holistic cancer coach and do Raindrops frequently on patients undergoing chemo. The rule of thumb is to keep the Raindrop for forty-eight hours on either side of the chemo days. It is not recommended for those undergoing radiation." The reason behind this suggestion is to allow the chemo to do what it is intended to do and allow the oils to do what they need to do. Both are very powerful in the body and we want to help the client get the best of what they've chosen. In regards to radiation, the frequency of radiation and the frequency of essential oils don't match or support each other. Radiation creates havoc in the body, and the body needs to deal with the toxic effects. Adding oils which may have an additional detoxing effect may be too much for the body to handle.

A bit of advice that I have carried with me and applied often when working with new clients diagnosed with cancer is from Marie Koepke, RN. She explained to me that a cancer patient's body is not dealing with detox well. When looking at it this way, it does not make sense to ask a body already having difficulty processing toxins to add essential oils, which will 'kick up' more toxins to be processed. Their body has difficulty processing toxins, why add oils that will overwhelm the system? Instead, use oils that will support the body with healing by choosing oils that are high in monoterpenes and sesquiterpenes.

Working with Receivers on a Cancer Journey:

I call this a "cancer journey" because when someone receives the diagnosis of cancer their path to changing this diagnosis starts. Each person has a unique journey because they may be presented with different options, they may research different alternatives, and the decision of what they do is dependent on many factors; such as, the type of cancer they have, their religious beliefs, their feeling towards western medicine, their current health, their family, their openness to holistic choices, insurance, etc. No one will make the same decisions, and each choice will then lead to a selection of new choices.

When I see clients in my office who have the diagnosis of cancer I put them in two general phases: receiving treatment and after treatment. In the following pages I would like to distinguish both of these phases and give some generalizations to help you support your Receivers while they are on their cancer journey.

Seeing Receivers During Cancer Treatments:

☐ Comfort

When someone is going through cancer treatments you may notice that they have a port in their upper chest, either on the right or left side (Picture #52). You should not massage the catheter or touch the port. In the picture, you can see the port under the skin and also the catheter laying over the clavicle. The catheter is inserted into the internal jugular vein or the subclavian vein. This port eliminates the need for the patient to get an IV in their arm when they receive chemotherapy or high-dose supplements. The location of the port does not pose an issue for giving Raindrop. When you balance your Receiver, your hands will be on their shoulders, so you will not be in contact with the port.

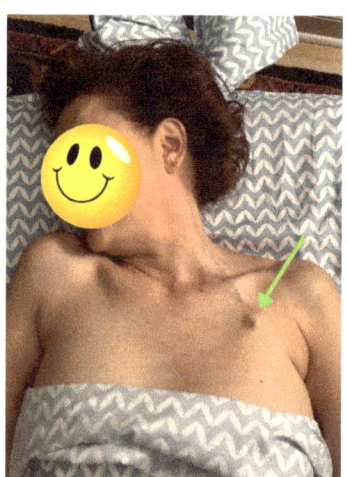

Picture # 52

Some people find that the port causes discomfort when they are lying prone. Simply ask your Receiver if the port is tender when they lie on their stomach, they will let you know right away. To take away that discomfort, use a soft wedge, small pillow, or towel to place between the port and massage table.

If someone is receiving Raindrops while they are going through cancer treatments, it is important for you to remember to be flexible. Treatments can make the area with cancer uncomfortable, sore and swollen. Your Receiver may be able to lie on their stomach during one session, but not the next. Side-lying may not even be an option. This is a good time to dig into your wellness toolbox and choose the tools that you have that would support your Receiver the best. A full Raindrop session may not be possible or even the best option.

During treatments, it is not uncommon for the patient to have some degree of swelling. Swelling may be due to the side effects of drugs, side effects of chemo, the body being over taxed, or due to heart, liver, or kidney weakness.

Swelling indicates that the lymphatic system is overtaxed. This is not a time to add phenols to the mix, especially if your Receiver is new to essential oils and Raindrop. Consider using oils that support oxygenation, are soothing, relaxing, and that support the lymphatic system.

As a wellness provider, it is important for you to know if the swelling is due to heart, liver, or kidney weakness as that will have a great impact on which wellness tools you can use with your Receiver. If there is weakness in the heart, liver, or kidneys then I suggest you first receive clearance from their doctor or naturopath to continue sessions. Using essential oils that will not tax the liver or kidneys is important, so focus on oils high in monoterpenes and sesquiterpenes.

☐ Emotional State

As I stated before, when someone gets the diagnosis of cancer, that starts their journey of many decisions. These choices come from the doctors with great speed and abundance with little time for the patient to make the choice.

A diagnosis often leads to the patient and/or family members doing a great deal of research and searching for second opinions and practitioners for alternative treatments. It is not uncommon for Receivers to do a great deal of traveling for alternative treatments.

This diagnosis often places a great deal of stress on not only the patient, but the whole family. There are numerous appointments, there may be traveling, missed work, missed income, and additional expenses.

It is safe to say that your Receivers who are in the treatment part of their cancer journey are generally feeling overwhelmed, scared, frustrated, and tired.

☐ Main Goals

Receivers who are seeing you for Raindrop during Cancer treatments often look for the physical benefits of relaxation, to sleep better, and to receive the support from the essential oils.

This is a wonderful time for Spiritual Healers to support these Receivers with emotional release and by teaching self-care skills to use at home and during treatments to support relaxation and coping skills.

After Cancer

☐ Comfort

If your Receiver went the traditional route for cancer, they may have undergone surgery, chemo, and perhaps radiation.

In my practice I have seen the long term physical and emotional impact of the traditional approach to cancer on and in my clients.

Surgery will always leave scars. Depending on where the surgery is and how it was done will determine where the scars are and which muscles are impacted. This may affect how your Receiver can lie on the massage table. You may need to have an extra pillow for women who have had breast surgery and/or reconstruction when they lie prone. Someone who had abdominal surgery may not be able to lie on their stomachs, and you may consider the side-lying position.

Talk with your Receiver and find out which position is the most comfortable for them to sleep at night. This will give you some ideas on what will work best for their positioning on the massage table. Radiation also has a long term effect on muscles and bones. Muscles and tissue that have been exposed to radiation for cancer treatment are changed. Muscles tend to get tight and tender, and bones become weak.

The combination of scar tissue and radiation has a huge impact on your Receiver's posture and muscular pain for a long time. It is estimated that tissue, which really is muscle, is impacted by radiation for ten years.

Often Receivers may unknowingly take on a "protective" posture for the area that was affected by cancer. After breast cancer, it is not uncommon to see a woman with her shoulder forward on the side which had the cancer and treatments. This learned posture, along with scar tissue, restricted movement, and radiation, causes the muscles to be extra tight, leading to a great deal of frustrating muscular pain.

☐ Emotional State

My Receivers often tell me that they are grateful that they have "made it to the other side" of cancer, but generally there is some level of anger, frustration, and fear to go along with that gratitude.

Most Receivers did not expect the scars, lymphedema, and muscular pain that are a direct result of the surgeries. These are life-long changes to their body that often have a daily impact on their lives.

My Receivers also shared with me the fear that tugs at them that the cancer may return one day. Though the cancer diagnosis may be gone, the physical and emotional scars are constantly there.

☐ Main Goals

After cancer, many Receivers are interested in Raindrop to support their health and detox.

Physically, Raindrop is a fantastic tool to help muscles to relax and ease muscular discomfort.

Emotionally Raindrop supports emotional release of fear, anger, and frustration.

Children

Depending on how big your kiddo is and how cuddly they are, you can use the adaptations for giving Raindrop to babies and toddlers for a long time.

For children, you will still decrease, dilute, and go slow. If this is a child's first time receiving oils on their back, then applying a base oil first is recommended. You will not be doing a full Raindrop session on a child, which is fine. Choose two to four oils that will support your goals.

Children usually receive Raindrops for respiratory support, immune support, digestive support, and relaxation.

Some kids will lie there and enjoy all the relaxing and stimulating tactile stimulation, while others will not. Just go with it and be flexible. Don't force it. Just remember, your primary goal is to get the oils on! With children, you are definitely going to be doing a 'Quickie Raindrop.' Any other gentle rubbing, finger circles, and spinal Vital Flex you get in is icing on the cake.

When working with minors you always want a parent or guardian in the room with you. This is a great opportunity for you to show the parent how to do the Raindrop.

It also is very important to follow up with the parent after the Raindrop to touch base on their observations and work through any questions or concerns they may have.

Cortisone Injections for Pain

People typically get cortisone or steroid injections to relieve joint pain. These shots reduce inflammation in the area and calm the nerves, which often reduces the pain. We want to remember when it comes to Raindrop in relation to these injections that the injection needs to stay in the body for a few days to do its job.

We don't want the essential oils from Raindrop to break down the steroid before it has the chance to complete its goal. The common recommendation for going back to exercise after the injection is three to ten days.

Massage is generally not recommended right after receiving a steroid or cortisone injection. Leaning towards the conservative side, it is a good idea to wait seven to fourteen days after the injection to do a Raindrop.

Digestive System

To support your Receiver's colon and get those exits working well, you can add some extra VitaFlex along with the colon points on the shin and soles of the feet (both of these locations and techniques are taught in CARE VitaFlex classes).

Tanya Schoessow also shared, "For those needing extra digestive support, after VitaFlexing the legs and feet, I'll apply a warm towel to the shins. The Receiver is given a huge WOW after."

Edema vs Lymphedema

When the body has trauma like a sprained ankle, a blow, or surgery, the area will swell. The swelling or edema is normal and is meant to protect the area and help it heal. In time, the body will naturally deal with this extra lymph and the swelling will go down.

When someone has had cancer and lymph nodes are removed, as often is done during breast cancer surgery, there will be swelling like one would experience from any type of surgery. If more lymph nodes are removed than the body can compensate for, then that swelling may become consistent. This is now considered lymphedema. This, unfortunately, is a common outcome of breast cancer treatments that include radiation, lumpectomy and/or surgery. This is a lifelong condition that often requires daily care.

When working with someone with swelling, it is important to remember that the lymphatic system is the cleansing system. If the swelling is short term and obviously due to an injury, then there is little concern that their lymphatic system is compromised. It is doing what it should do.

If the swelling is consistent, then that shows there is some sort of compromise in this Receiver's lymphatic system. We may not know what is causing this compromise, but the consistent swelling lets us know that they may have some challenge in detoxing. I highly suggest reducing the amount of oils used. Consider using oils that also support the lymphatic system.

Emotional Release and Trauma Response

Emotional Release:

We know that Raindrop has the ability to create an environment that makes it rich for emotional release. As we educate our Receiver before their first Raindrop experience, practitioners need to mention to the Receiver that they may experience an emotional release during or after their session.

I find that when my Receiver has a physical goal for their session, they get nervous about the possibility of having an emotional release. That is why when I explain emotional release to them, I try to take the fear away.

Those who come to their Raindrop session with an emotional release goal are open to the possibility of a release. The most common concern I hear from this group is, "Once I start releasing, I'm afraid I will not be able to stop!"

To immediately alleviate some common concerns and answer the usual questions, I've come up with my "Emotional Release Chat" below. You are welcome to use whatever fits for you.

The Emotional Release Chat:

"The oils are great at dislodging toxins from our body. Besides chemical toxins, one of the toxins we may be holding on to are negative emotions. If an emotion is released, that just means that your body is ready to let go of that emotion. If you feel like crying, feel angry, or start to think about something you have not thought of for a long time, that may indicate a release.

Don't worry, if you cry while on the massage table you are in good company. Many clients have used this time to release and they are surprised how light they feel afterwards.

Sometimes if someone is holding on to an emotion, one way their body lets us know it is ready to release is through a tingling or unusual sensation in a particular location, like the knee or throat. If that happens, let me know and then I can tailor the oil choice or offer you an affirmation to repeat to help your body to easily release."

For those that express a fear that they may keep on releasing indefinitely I'll mention, "Your spirit is so smart, as it will only allow one emotion to be released at a time. As we get closer to the end of our session I'll let you know that we will be closing the session. I'll also use essential oils to ground you, so you will not be sobbing as you walk out the door–don't worry!"

Most of my clients like the idea of an Emotional Release Raindrop and often release after the session. I explain to my concerned clients that it is common for these clients to share that they had their release when they had some time to themselves, like in the shower or the following day when the kids were at school, or even in a dream.

If your Raindrop practice has an emotional/spiritual focus you probably have your "emotional release" talk down. If you have a physical Raindrop practice you still need to mention to your Receiver the potential for emotional release so they don't get anxious if they have one.

Trauma Response:

Crying and sighing are all associated with emotional release and Raindrop Practitioners are familiar with those signs.

But what about a trauma response? What is it and how can you tell if your Receiver is having a trauma response and not an emotional release?

Trauma is a big topic, though it is something we don't often discuss. Raindroppers need to keep in mind that we've all experienced trauma. It could be a big trauma or a small trauma, but either one can have a lasting impact on us.

A trauma response is not the same as an emotional release, though emotional release may be a tool to help heal the trauma. During a trauma response, the nervous system is responding to the trigger (sensation, word, event, smell) in the same way that it did during the original traumatic event. If the past event caused the person to respond with anxiety, stress, or withdrawal, that is the same nervous system response that will happen when they are exposed to that trigger again. The body response can be seen when your receiver is extra fidgety, shifting their body often, clenching their fists, or zoning out.

What was interesting to learn about trauma response is that the person experiencing the response often does not connect their current body response to their past traumas. This can leave the individual confused as they wonder why everyone else loves Raindrop, but for them it creates such stress or anxiety.

People who love the Raindrop Technique tend to love all parts of it; the smell of the different oils and how the techniques range from a light tickle on the back to firm VitaFlex on the feet. As a practitioner, we need to remember that the aromas and touches that feel good to us, may bring back a traumatic memory for others, resulting in a trauma or nervous system response. Combining all those smells and touches in an hour session may be too activating for some, causing them to become overwhelmed.

My friend and teacher, Dawn Petek helped me understand the difference between an emotional release and a trauma response.

In a class Dawn taught, she explained how she became overstimulated during a Raindrop, causing her to shut down. In time, she realized that feeling like she was in a vulnerable position (lying face down) along with the physical sensations from the Raindrop triggered trauma from her past which caused her to feel frozen (her nervous system response to the original trauma).

From her experience, Dawn now asks her Raindrop Receivers if they have a history of trauma. This allows the Receiver to respond with a simple "yes" or "no," or explain more if they want.

This is a question you may want to add to the Eight Questions you ask your new Raindrop Receivers. If your Receiver answers "yes" to this question, then it is a good idea to explain that when we're holding on to negative emotions from past traumas, we may feel the intense physical sensations associated with the original nervous system response if there is a trigger that activates the body memory. It's important for both you and the Receiver to be extra observant of their body language during the session. It is through body language that you'll most likely pick up if they are experiencing a trauma response from their session.

If it looks like your Receiver is having a trauma response because they are super fidgety, you can simply apply a grounding essential oil like Grounding® blend, Gathering® blend, or galbanum to their heels or back of their neck and encourage them to inhale it.

It can be difficult to determine if your Receiver is shutting down or just very relaxed and sleeping. If you are not sure, check in and listen to how they respond. If they sound distant and removed from their bodies, it could be a trauma response.

When a Receiver gets up from your table after a Raindrop, they usually look relaxed, calm, and sleepy. They also tend to look relaxed even after an emotional release. They may comment about how great they feel after this release.

When someone gets off the massage table and they look stressed, anxious, or have the "deer in headlights" look, then that is most likely a trauma response. Use the same grounding essential oils applied to heels and their neck. Encouraging deep breathing of the oil will also help your Receiver.

If you see a trauma response occur in your Receiver, then please consider sharing more information about trauma and emotional release, and refer them to Dawn's website (DawnPetek.com) to learn more.

As Raindrop Practitioners, we need to remember to be mindful of our Receiver's body language before, during, and after the session. This is true for sessions that have a physical or emotional/spiritual goal. Our role is to apply oils, stay observant of our Receiver's emotional and physical responses, and be open to any intuitive information we may receive. The attitude of "just getting one more session in today" does not fit for one offering Raindrop in their wellness practice.

Multiple Sclerosis (MS) and Other Conditions Affecting the Myelin Sheath

What happens with MS is that the myelin sheath that covers the nerve gets inflamed, which causes scars. This damage to the myelin sheath results in a poor connection or no connection between the Central Nervous System and muscles served by the affected nerve.

Heat makes MS symptoms worse by further reducing the ability of the nerves to conduct electrical impulses. Instead of applying a moist heat pack at the end of Raindrop, apply a cool or cold pack.

If you are not sure or feel guilty about putting a cool pack on your Receiver, ask them a simple question: "Do you prefer to take hot or cool showers?" Their response will guide you in what temperature pack to use.

Neuropathy

I have had a few Receivers who had neuropathy from chemotherapy who noticed that the neuropathy decreased after VitaFlexing the Raindrop oils on the spinal points of their feet.

Clients have shared that the pain, numbing, and the "feeling like I'm walking on pebbles" decreased.

Nursing

There are three questions that nursing mamas ask when it comes to nursing and Raindrop:

1. Will the peppermint in Raindrop reduce her milk production?
2. Will the oils change the taste of her milk?
3. Will the detox from the Raindrop, and the toxins go into her milk?

Let's address each concern.

"Will peppermint reduce my milk?"

There is a 50/50 chance that peppermint will reduce a nursing mama's milk. If my Receiver is a new mama and she is anxious about the possibility of reducing her milk, then I simply omit peppermint and use another oil instead like rosemary or copaiba. My philosophy is why cause any more stress for a new mom?

If the Receiver is an experienced mama and is open to testing out how her body responds to peppermint when nursing, I'll use it. It is important to educate Mama and leave the decision entirely up to her.

"Will the oils change the taste of my milk?"

When used in Raindrop, I feel that essential oils will add a slight flavor to Mama's milk. Any foods we eat will affect the quality, color, and taste of our milk!

When I was nursing and giving Raindrops, my girls never turned up her nose at my milk, even when giving or receiving a Raindrop. Many nursing mamas have reported that their baby did not slow down nursing after Mama had her Raindrop. Actually, once my girls started eating solid foods, they enjoyed a wide variety of flavors and spices. I wonder if my essential oil use contributed to their being open to a wide range of flavors.

If there is still a concern, then Mama should be encouraged to do a small test. She can apply some of the more flavorful oils like oregano, thyme, and basil to her feet and see how the baby responds when nursing a few hours later. Perhaps she just experiences Foot VitaFlex with all the Raindrop oils and then observes the baby's nursing behavior for the next day or two. After these tests, Mama can then make an informed and confident decision about receiving a full Raindrop.

"If I detox from Raindrop, will the toxins go into my milk?"

Sadly, since we have been exposed to so many toxins throughout the years, toxins have been found in breast milk. But, having a Raindrop does not mean your body will dispose of the toxins your body releases through your breast milk.

Since the mammary glands and lymph nodes are so close to each other in the breast tissue and axillary region (underarm), people seem to worry that they are similar systems or will easily mix, which is not the case at all! Your body eliminates toxins through the lymphatic system, and a nursing mama produces milk in mammary glands.

Mammary glands are enlarged and modified sweat glands–hollow cavities (alveoli) lined with milk-secreting cells. Mammary glands are regulated by Mama's hormones and the endocrine system, NOT the lymphatic system.

The lymphatic system is an open system. It is made of liquid that bathes all our cells. The lymph's job is to collect large molecules like toxins, dead cells, and bacteria and carry these into the lymph vessels. Lymph vessels travel from fingers and toes to the heart. Along the lymph vessels are lymph nodes, where white blood cells wait to attack and destroy what was brought into the lymph vessels. Lymph nodes are part of the lymphatic system; they are NOT part of the endocrine system.

Even though lymph nodes and mammary glands both look like little hollow balls and are found in the breast, they are not regulated by the same system. If Mama detoxed from Raindrop, there is no reason for Mama's body to eliminate toxins through her breast milk; her lymph system would do that job.

Should Mama go on a big detox while nursing? I don't think that is a wise idea because her body needs more calories and nutrition to produce enough milk. Paying attention to the quality and purity of her food while pregnant and nursing is the best choice.

Staying hydrated by drinking lots of water is the best way to support Mama's lymphatic system.

Asking the right questions and making adjustments if needed are still appropriate for a nursing mama.

Obesity

When a Receiver is obese we need to remember two things pertaining to Raindrop. The first is that toxins are stored in fat cells. The more toxins someone has, the more fat cells the body will produce. As toxins are released, people often find themselves losing weight without making any other changes in their lives. If your Receiver is coming to you and has not made an effort to change the amount of toxins they are exposed to, then speaking in general terms, they probably have a lot of toxins to release. Going slow and reducing the amount of oils, especially the phenols, is important for this Receiver.

Physically, Raindrop can support toxin release. Often, obese clients complain of sore backs and painful joints which can be helped with Raindrop.

Emotionally, obese clients are often holding on to negative emotions about their weight or emotions which are the cause of their extra weight.

Pregnancy

In time, that 'baby bump' makes it uncomfortable and even unsafe for mama to lie on her stomach. After twenty-two weeks Mama should not lie on her back for longer than five minutes. After thirteen weeks, Mama should not lie on her stomach for longer than five minutes. This means that Mama needs to lie on her side for Raindrop. You'll find detailed information on how to help Mama get comfortable side-lying on a massage table in Chapter Ten. The best side for her to lie on is her left, as that positioning will allow Mama's heart to function better, which leads to the most oxygen to be delivered to the baby.

There are many views on whether one should receive a Raindrop when pregnant. I determine my answer based on how much essential oil the expecting mom used before becoming pregnant. If she did not use oils before pregnancy, my thought is, why introduce a bunch of oils at one time (as in Raindrop) now? Why not see if there are one or two oils she can use to help her find the support she is looking for? Most expecting moms are looking for support with their digestive system, muscular system, immune system, or with sleep. This is where the book *Gentle Babies* by Debra Rayburn will help you find out which oils or supplements could be helpful and appropriate.

When I was pregnant, I gave Raindrops and taught CARE classes through all nine months. Now that was a lot of essential oil I was exposing myself and my energetic baby to, but I felt comfortable doing so. I had been exposed to that amount of oils for years before pregnancy. My body was used to the oils. In fact, the only time during my nine months of pregnancy that I did not have morning sickness was when I was giving a Raindrop!!

In my practice, I have a personal rule that if a mama is new to Raindrop, then I will not do a Raindrop on her in the first trimester. This is a delicate time, and if anything were to happen, I would not want her to have any thoughts at all that Raindrop or oils could have been the cause.

You may consider using a 'System Supporting Raindrop' if needed or using singles or blends that would support and prepare a mama for giving birth. I feel strongly that when doubting if an oil should or should not be used, the mama has the final say.

A pregnant woman can receive Raindrops, but we need to adapt a few things for a mama. The adaptations will depend on which stage of pregnancy she is in. Not only do we need to look at the oils that are used, but we also need to adapt how she lies when she receives her Raindrop.

Lying Face Up

The guidance I share is from Carol Osborne-Sheets from her book *Pre- and Perinatal Massage Therapy*. Her recommendation is that once a woman has reached twenty-two weeks of her pregnancy, she should not lie on her back for an extended period of time. Carol says "extended" is more than five minutes!

Her reasoning for why mamas should not be lying on their backs for over five minutes is because the weight of the fetus could be putting pressure on the super vena cava, which is the main vein for bringing the blood back to the mama's heart. If there is compression on the vein, not only will it affect Mom's blood pressure, but also the baby's.

Carol's other reason for recommending that Mama not lie on her back at this stage of pregnancy is because it can cause lower back pain. This means that we need to adapt how we offer this mama Foot VitaFlex!

Lying Face Down

Carol also recommends that once mothers reach thirteen weeks, then they should not lie prone, or on their stomachs for a long period of time, more than five minutes.

In *Pre- and Perinatal Massage Therapy*, Carol explains that even though mamas may lie on their stomach when sleeping, they should not lie on their stomachs on a massage table.

Her first reason is that when you compare the firmness of a bed versus a typical massage table, there is a big difference in their hardness and how much they "give." Massage tables, even with padding, are going to be more firm and have less give than a bed.

Her second reason is that when you are lying on a bed sleeping, no one is putting pressure on your back. Even with Raindrop, we do put some pressure on Mama's back.

This means that we will need to adapt the second half of Raindrop for mamas, when Receivers are lying face down and the techniques are done on the back.

When I'm working with a pregnant woman, I always err on the safe side. I choose to make adaptations for Mama's positioning on the massage table for the whole Raindrop experience. That means that after twenty-two weeks of pregnancy she will not be lying on her back for Foot VitaFlex, or after thirteen weeks of pregnancy she won't be lying on her stomach for the second half of Raindrop.

You may have seen the nifty pregnancy pillows just for massaging women when they are pregnant. The pillows have cutouts for swollen breasts and bellies. The idea is with these cutouts in the pillow, mama can comfortably lie face down on a massage table without her belly getting in the way. I'm not a fan of these pregnancy pillows, and neither is Carol. She explains that when a pregnant mama lies face down on one of these pillows, it causes further strain on the taxed uterine ligaments.

Another consideration is that these pregnancy pillows are super expensive. There is no need for this extra expense. You can set up mama to be toasty and comfortable with the adaptations I share with you here.

It is recommended that mama lie on her left side. Lying on the left allows for the best cardiac function for the mom, which will give the baby the most oxygen.

As a professional Wellness Provider, it is imperative that you know when it is time for your pregnant Receivers to stop lying prone or supine and change to side-lying. This is not a pregnancy massage and should not be regarded as such. This is simply applying the oils in the Raindrop Technique for a pregnant woman.

Scoliosis

A common question I receive is: "If someone has scoliosis, should I do the techniques to follow their spine, or should I do the techniques in the middle of their back where the spine should be?"

Follow their spine. It is the best way to stimulate the nerves exiting the spine.

CHAPTER FIFTEEN
A Growing Resource

Thank you so much for purchasing this book. I hope that you found the information in here valuable. My goal is to help you be more confident working with a wide range of Raindrop Receivers so that you can offer support to more people while growing your wellness practice into a thriving business.

Your experience is valuable and I would love to be able to share your "Golden Raindrop Nugget of Wisdom" with others. If you have a tool, resource, class, "Golden Nugget," or technique that you feel other Raindroppers would find helpful please let me know! You can contact me on my website at AdaptingRaindrop.com

Acknowledgments

Thank you Holy Spirit for the insights and gentle nudges during this time of healing and helping.

I'm so thankful to all of those who so willingly shared their wisdom with me and other Raindroppers.

Much love and appreciation to my husband Brian and daughter Joy for their support and encouragement during this book writing process.

Thank you Dawn Petek and Sherian McCoy for your time and added insight.

Many thanks to Kaycee Lallatin for her fantastic editing skills.

My thanks again to Steve Stryker for the beautiful cover photo.

References

Hagan, C. G. (2022). *The Raindrop Resource Guide for Oily Families: Confidently Adapt Raindrop to Fit Your Receiver's Current Needs*. Your HealthySteps.

Harrison, J. (2018). *Easy Essential Oil Chemistry: Unlock the Healing Potential of Essential Oils*. Flower of Life Press.

McCraw, J. (2021). *The Pathway to Emotional Healing*. Wellspring Health.

Mein, C. L. (1998). *Releasing Emotional Patterns with Essential Oils*. Amsterdam University Press.

Osborne-Sheets, C. (1998). *Pre and Perinatal Massage Therapy: A Comprehensive Practioners' Guide to Pregnancy, Labor, Postpartum* (1st ed.). Body Therapy Assoc.

Price, S and Price L (2007). *Aromatherapy for Health Professionals*. (3rd ed.). Churchill Lingstone

Ph.D., S. K. (1998). *Advanced Aromatherapy: The Science of Essential Oil Therapy* (US ed.). Healing Arts Press.

Raybern, D. (2022). *Gentle Babies Essential OIls and Natural Remedies for Pregnancy, Childbirth and Infant Care* (4th ed.). Growing Healthy Homes LLC.

Schnaubelt, K. (1999). *Medical Aromatherapy: Healing with Essential Oils*. Frog Books.

Schnaubelt, K. (2011). *The Healing Intelligence of Essential Oils: The Science of Advanced Aromatherapy*. Healing Arts Press.

Stewart, D. (2005). *Chemistry of Essential Oils Made Simple: God's Love Manifest in Molecules* (6.8.2005). N A P S A C Reproductions.

Young, D. G. (2003a). *Essential Oils Integrative Medical Guide: Building Immunity, Increasing Longevity, and Enhancing Mental Performance With Therapeutic-Grade Essential Oils*. Yl Wisdom Llc.

Young, D. G. (2003b). *Raindrop Technique*. Yl Wisdom Llc.

More Raindrop Education at AdaptingRaindrop.com

Pain-Free Raindrop

How to Stand and Move when giving a Raindrop so YOUR body doesn't hurt.

Technique Intentions

When you Understand the Purpose, You Can Do it Better

All Things Raindrop Membership

The Digital Reference for Raindrop.

Christina G. Hagan, LMBT, LCCI, M.Ed.

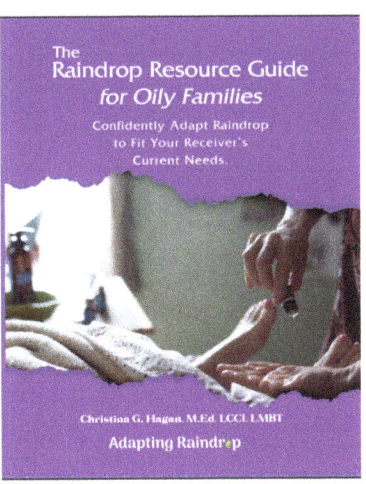

Coming Soon *"The Practitioners' Corner"*

Author Bio

Christina G. Hagan, LMBT, LCCI, M.Ed, is a licensed massage therapist and fully certified instructor with the Center for Aromatherapy Research and Education. She has been teaching and offering the Raindrop Technique since 2006.

Her goal is to support you in your Raindrop journey so that you can feel confident offering this flexible and effective technique to a wide variety of Raindrop Receivers.

During her free time, Christina loves spending time with her family on a hike, swimming in the lake or gardening.

Thank You For Reading My Book!

I really appreciate all of your feedback and I love hearing what you have to say.

I need your input to make the next version of this and and my future books better.

Please take two minutes now to leave a helpful review where you purchased this book.   You also are welcome to send me an email.

Thanks so much!

Christina Hagan   :)

www.ingramcontent.com/pod-product-compliance
Ingram Content Group UK Ltd.
Pitfield, Milton Keynes, MK11 3LW, UK
UKHW062045180426
11947UKWH00030B/2056